67 Ways To Do the Works of Mercy with Your Kids

Heidi Indahl

W0010585

Our Sunday Visitor
www.osv.com

Nihil obstat: Rev. Timothy Hall
Censor librorum
September 22, 2018

Imprimatur: †Most Rev. John M. Quinn
Bishop of Winona
September 22, 2018

Acknowledgments continue on page 96.

Book design by Jerry Windley-Daoust. Development editing by Regina Lordan, Barbara Allaire, and Jerry Windley-Daoust. Copyediting by Karen Lynn Carter.

ISBN: 978-1-68192-530-1 (Inventory No. T2419)
LCCN: 2019943193

PRINTED IN THE UNITED STATES OF AMERICA

Contents

8   Introduction: An Invitation to Do the Works of Mercy

    8   Parents Provide the Foundation for a Lifelong
            Commitment of Service

    9   Passing on a Passion for Service

    10   Take the First Step

    12   Q & A: How to Use This Book

17   PART 1: PREPARING

18   A Crash Course in Christian Service

    18   What Is Christian Service?

    20   A Christian Approach to Service

21   Addressing Barriers to Service

25   Talking about the Tough Stuff

    26   Sheltering the Homeless

    27   Visiting the Imprisoned

    29   Visiting the Sick

    30   Feeding the Hungry, Giving Drink to the Thirsty

    32   Clothing the Naked

    34   Burying the Dead

37   Building a Culture of Service at Home

    37   Care for Siblings

43   Feed the Hungry, Give Drink to the Thirsty, Clothe the Naked

43   Make a blessing box (3+, 7+, 13+)

43   Plant an extra row (3+, 7+, 13+)

44   Make a meal for a family with a new baby or for a family in crisis (7+, 13+)

45   Serve at a soup kitchen, community meal, food shelf, or donation center ($, 7+, 13+)

45   Organize a food drive (3+, 7+, 13+)

45   Feed community helpers (3+, 7+, 13+)

46   Sheltering the Homeless

46   Serve with Family Promise (7+, 13+)

47   Pack a bag for a child in foster care (7+, 13+)

47   Visit or help a homeless shelter (7+, 13+)

48   Sleep out for the homeless (13+)

48   Help a ReStore (7+, 3+)

49   Disaster-related assistance (13+)

49   "Adopt" a college student (3+, 7+, 13+)

50   Sponsor a refugee or immigrant family with your parish (3+, 7+, 13+)

51   Visit the Sick

51   Take care of kids in need (3+, 7+, 13+)

52   Provide respite care and friendship (E, $, 3+, 7+, 13+)

53   Serve the women religious in your community (3+, 7+, 13+)

53   Advocate for the unborn (E, $, 3+, 7+, 13+)

54 Work with a nursing home or senior facility
(E, $, 3+, 7+, 13+)

55 Make a blanket for someone undergoing chemotherapy
treatments (3+, 7+, 13+)

56 Be a reading or study buddy ($, 13+)

57 Visit the Imprisoned

57 Be a mother's helper (E, $, 13+)

57 Spring and fall yard cleanup (E, $,7+, 13+)

58 Visit and bring a homemade gesture in collaboration with
Eucharistic ministry (E, $, 3+, 7+, 13+)

58 Give kids a safe place to play (7+, 13+)

58 Drive someone to church (E, $, 3+, 7+, 13+)

59 Work with your diocese to help a family who has an
incarcerated parent ($, 13+)

59 Take on human trafficking and child labor (E, 7+, 13+)

60 Carol at a prison or court-ordered rehabilitation facility
($, 7+, 13+)

60 Visit a homebound person (E, $, 3+, 7+, 13+)

60 Meals on Wheels

61 Improve access to healthy food, clean water, and
opportunity (3+, 7+, 13+)

63 Bury the Dead

63 Serve a funeral meal (E, $, 3+, 7+, 13+)

64 Honor a baby who has died (E, $, 7+, 13+)

65 Care for Our Common Home

65 Reduce, reuse, recycle (E, $, 3+, 7+, 13+)

66 Beautify your community (E, $, 3+, 7+, 13+)

68 Create a creation care team in your family and/or with
your parish ($, 7+, 13+)

69   Visit a farmers' market (E, 3+, 7+, 13+)

69   Collect scrap metal to collect money for charity (E, $, 13+)

70   Adding to Our Gifts with Prayer

70   Holy hour for religious liberty (E, $, 3+, 7+, 13+)

70   Pray for priests (E, $, 3+, 7+, 13+)

70   Pray for foreign missionaries (E, $, 3+, 7+, 13+)

71   Serve your parish ($, 7+, 13+)

72   Serve without Leaving Home

72   Teach a new skill (E, $, 7+, 13+)

72   Host a party for a charity (E, $, 3+, 7+, 13+)

72   Write a letter (E, $, 3+, 7+, 13+)

74   Clean closets and donate (E, $, 7+, 13+)

74   Send a care package (E, 3+, 7+, 13+)

75   Stuff a stocking (3+, 7+, 13+)

76   Random acts of electronic kindness (E, $, 13+)

77   Organize a new project on DoSomething.org (13+)

78   PART III: REFLECTING

79   Immediate Intentional Reflection

80   Reflect Throughout the Liturgical Year

80   Celebrate a liturgical season (E, $, 3+, 7+)

82   Praying it Forward

82   Catholic Social Teaching

85   Building Community through Service

86   Make a neighborhood map and directory
(E, $, 3+, 7+, 13+)

86   Organize a neighborhood party (3+, 7+, 13+)

87   Form a babysitting co-op (E, $, 13+)

87   Welcome the stranger (E, $, 3+, 7+, 13+)

88   Go trick-or-treating in your neighborhood
(E, $, 3+, 7+, 13+)

88   Christmas caroling (E, $, 3+, 7+, 13+)

88   Community service days (3+, 7+, 13+)

89   Neighborhood watch (E, $, 13+)

90   Start a Service Club

91   Final Thoughts

92   APPENDIX: RESOURCES

92   Books

94   Websites

95   Online Articles

96   ACKNOWLEDGMENTS

Introduction: An Invitation to Do the Works of Mercy

Perhaps as a child you had to memorize the works of mercy, inspired by the parable of the sheep and the goats in Matthew 25: feed the hungry, give drink to the thirsty, clothe the naked, and so on. Before we dive into the nitty-gritty of doing the works of mercy and all kinds of service with your kids, I would like to briefly share the story of how I came to be so passionate about this. It's a story I often refer to as my "journey of service," because doing the works of mercy (or any form of service) is an ongoing process of growth, not just an isolated action. My story might also help you better understand the philosophy behind the ideas in the rest of this book.

Parents Provide the Foundation for a Lifelong Commitment of Service

I am an adult convert to the Catholic faith. I grew up in a Protestant family, with my mom working as a children's minister in and around churches for most of my formative years. As much as I love my Catholic faith, I must credit my Protestant upbringing for my love of Scripture and service. My parents made sure our whole family regularly served others in an intentional way. My mom was always organizing service opportunities at church; our family participated in many of these, but we also performed service activities on our own.

Often our acts of Christian service weren't big deals. If someone had a small need that we could meet, we did, simply because we could. If we saw that the food donation bin at church was running low, we dropped a few cans in. We picked up extra cans and boxes of food that were on sale so we would have them on hand for this purpose.

We also spent a lot of time engaged in larger acts of service that left a lasting impression on me. I can still picture the industrial warehouse in a rundown area of town that was home to Sharing & Caring Hands, a Twin Cities–based ministry for those in need. We kids used to help sort bags of clothing that filled an entire room; we'd climb the huge piles and take out stuff that was especially silly or gross. (Who donates used underwear?)

Twenty years later, I read an article about the founder of Sharing & Caring Hands, Mary Jo Copeland, who had been invited to meet with Pope Francis during his 2015 visit to the United States. The article detailed the history of her ministry and how it had grown to serve many thousands of people in need. As I read the article, I realized that my own family, along with countless other families and individuals, had contributed to that legacy. Without them, thousands of people might not have received the help they needed.

It was these early experiences that nurtured a passion for the works of mercy in my heart. As I moved into my teen years, I began to serve less with my parents and more with my friends. I traveled on Youthworks trips to sites around the United States and Mexico, and I worked food, clothing, and Christmas drives with my high school band. As a young adult, I was always actively serving in at least one or two areas; I never lost that feeling that this is just what people do.

I noticed, too, that even though my sister and I were spending less time doing the works of mercy with my parents, they were spending no less time serving on their own. Now, instead of packing Operation Christmas Child boxes with us, they were showing up at the packing facility to load semi-trailer trucks the day after Thanksgiving while everyone else was rushing to the stores. Now they were joining Habitat for Humanity weekend builds and encouraging my grandparents to do the same. The message this sent was clear: My parents served not just because it was good for us kids, but because it was good for them, too. They genuinely cared about other people.

Passing on a Passion for Service

I'm a parent now, with seven children, ages 0-14, and I've been thinking more about what I can do to instill this attitude in my own children. My ongoing conversion to Christ has been steeped in Christian service; I truly believe that my kids benefit from that, just as I did from my parents' lives of service.

Like my parents before me, my husband and I have tried to act in a way that is generous to our fellow human beings, but we also realize just how much is always left to do. We have moved a lot and haven't had the opportunity to get involved with any one group on a regular basis. Also, our life circumstances have made it sometimes feel as though we are more often the recipients of service than the givers.

Of our seven living children, three have special medical needs. Several years ago we had a house fire and lost almost all of our worldly possessions. In addition to three miscarriages, we have also had a stillbirth and an infant pass away shortly after birth. These times of being on the "other side" of need have shaped my own attitude toward serving others. Receiving the caring love of others has the potential to be a source of spiritual growth as much as serving others does.

Take the First Step

How can we help our children experience the incredible blessings that come from being the answer to someone else's prayers? This book is, at its core, the way that my husband and I have responded to this question. It is designed to help families get started on their journey of service by taking one step at a time, no matter how small.

My husband works an often-demanding job. We homeschool. I'm an author in my "spare" time. How on earth do we do all of this stuff? The simple answer is we don't. At least not all the time.

No bad solution exists to the problem of creating a culture of service in your family. Indeed, our great call as Christians is to love and to serve one another. Christ, through the Church, has called us to this great mission, and it is our job to respond with the how.

Over time, I have learned that it is always a mistake to treat service as either a to-do list item or a debit-credit system. This creates an obligatory system where people are compelled to serve and/or are demanding of service. A system or attitude of service without the virtue of humility doesn't work. What works is to step out in faith to serve those around us with no thought of repayment, while taking on faith that when our time comes someone else will avail themselves to take care of us.

This is not easy. It is not easy to be vulnerable. It is not easy to put ourselves into situations that are unfamiliar and uncomfortable, with people who are different from ourselves. It is not easy to know when obvious service might need to take a backseat as other priorities demand your family's attention.

I want this text to serve as a springboard for your family to develop a new definition of what it means to serve as a family. A new way of thinking not of barriers, but of possibilities. Service is not an action you can finish, but an attitude you can acquire.

By engaging in intentional active service projects such as those in this book, our family has developed an attitude of service that results in what I call accidental service. While homebound with children, I often forget that the little things help: Sewing new pillows for a friend's preschool classroom, taking time to share a phone call with an extended family member, encouraging letter writing (my daughter's favorite). We send a gift card for a meal after surgery instead of making a meal myself. These things are service too, and they are service opportunities that come to us regardless of circumstances.

I have designated an entire section of this text to the idea of serving others without leaving home, and I hope that as a reader you will find it both helpful and encouraging if you feel you are not in a place right now to engage your family outside of the home (p. 72).

I will explain how to use this book in the next section. For now, I want to leave you with these key insights from my own story:

1. The benefits of doing the works of mercy (or any form of Christian service) are enormous. It has been said so often that it is almost a cliché: People who serve others often end up getting more than they give, in spiritual and emotional terms. Teaching your kids to serve will provide them with enormous benefits throughout their lives.

2. Parents have a tremendous impact on their kids. If helping others is important to you, and you act on that value, then you have already taken an important step in teaching kids to serve.

3. Doing the works of mercy is a lifelong journey. That is because routinely giving yourself in service to others leads to insights and spiritual growth that change the way you serve. Taking time to discuss and reflect on your experience is key, a point that we will touch on more in part III on reflecting.

Are you ready to take that first step on your journey?
Then let's get started.

Q & A: How to Use This Book

Q: Why do the works of mercy with kids?

Why should parents make doing the works of mercy a family priority? Here are four reasons to consider.

1. Kids who serve others with their families are more likely to serve others in adulthood.

If it's important to you that your children grow up to be helpful adults who spend time serving others, then giving them lots of opportunities to serve others now is the best thing you can do.

John Roberto, writing in his article, "Best Practices in Family Faith Formation," cites a Search Institute study of 217,000 sixth- to twelfth-grade youth in public schools. The study found that "youth who say their parents 'spent lots of time helping others' are almost twice as likely themselves to serve others."

In many ways, this is common sense proven by research. When we do good things as a family, good things happen. Children who have done something, no matter how small, to help a person in need gain an understanding of human dignity without having to listen to long lectures; they have seen it and they know it, even if they can't define it. Acts of service help all of us, children and adults, develop a lens of compassion through which we can view the world.

As a bonus, service activities help kids develop leadership and collaboration skills.

2. Service honors God.

Loving others through acts of service is an integral part of a mature faith, not simply an extra for our spare time. Both the Bible and the teaching tradition of the Church emphasize this. As Jesus said, "Whatever you did for one of these least brothers of mine, you did for me" (Matthew 25:40). The works of mercy are a way to love God by loving one another.

The dignity of every human being, from conception until death, is the foundation of Catholic social teaching. Every human being possesses this God-given dignity because every person is loved by God: those who are homeless, children, the elderly, those imprisoned, the disabled, soldiers, teen moms … every one of us, no matter our condition.

3. Serving others nurtures a lively, lifelong faith.

Serving others is a powerful way to nurture a personal and meaningful faith in your children that they can carry into adulthood.

"Engaging in service with one's family can be a powerful opportunity for growing in faith," says Roberto, summarizing research on the topic. "Both children and adults are more likely to have a growing, strong faith when their family serves others together." In each act of service, we enhance our faith by living it. Through service we show, rather than tell, our children that each member of our society has dignity.

4. When your kids help others, others are more likely to help your kids.

When your kids regularly serve others, they become part of a community of service, the seed of what St. John Paul II called a "civilization of love." They build relationships with other generous people and with the people they serve. All those relationships may benefit your kids someday when they are the ones in need of help. A community woven together by love, respect, and mutual service is one of the most valuable assets you can give your kids.

Remember that the first steps on your family's journey of service don't need to be huge. This book includes lots of ideas, including many that are easy to pull off without a big investment.

Q: What will I find in this book?

The goal of this book is to make serving others with the members of your family fun, simple, and useful. It is divided into three main parts: Preparing, Acting, and Reflecting. These follow what I call the Cycle of Service. It is a cycle because each act of service prepares us to do another; and it is a cycle rather than a circle because each successive act of service brings new insights and opportunities for growth that affect the way we serve the next time. This is especially true when we take the time to intentionally reflect on our experience of service.

Here, then, are the three parts of this book that reflect the Cycle of Service:

Part I: Preparing. This section lays the groundwork for your family's journey of service and provides support along the way. It includes these short articles:

A Crash Course in the Works of Mercy and Christian Service. Read this for background on the works of mercy, Christian service, and where to go for more information on Catholic social teaching.

Addressing Barriers to Doing the Works of Mercy. What if serving others is difficult for our family? Here I discuss some of the obstacles preventing families from doing service together in a more intentional way. I can't promise easy answers, but I will offer some strategies to consider.

Talking about the Tough Stuff. This section provides background on some issues related to the works of mercy, as well as recommendations for other helpful resources. You can use these discussion resources to prepare your kids for a new service experience (e.g., going to a nursing home or a homeless shelter) or to help them process questions they might be struggling with after their service experience.

Building a Culture of Helping in the Family. You don't need to leave home to begin teaching your kids to serve; indeed, service at home fosters a culture of helping and prepares children to serve others in the wider community. Here, we talk about practical ways kids can help around the house.

Part II: Acting. The next section contains service ideas and strategies for carrying them out with kids. The ideas are grouped into themed sections roughly corresponding to the works of mercy. One way to use this book would be simply to pick it up and flip through it for service ideas ... or just open to the section that sounds appealing to your family and start there.

Your family may try and enjoy many of these activities. But you may not even have access to a number of them. You may try some only once. A few of the ideas may become regular habits or traditions for your family. Make it your goal to try out as many types of service as possible, enabling your family to find the kind of service that is the best fit for you. The more activities you try, the more likely that an attitude of service will take root in the heart of your family.

Many of the service ideas include references to Scripture, Catholic teaching, or the wisdom of the saints, as well as suggestions for additional resources.

The following key will help direct you to the activities that are most appealing and appropriate for your situation:

E   Easy
3+ Appropriate for 3–6-year-old children
7+ Appropriate for 7–12-year-old children
13+ Appropriate for teenagers
$ Indicates an activity that does not cost money

Most, though not all, of the activities, tie directly back to one of the corporal works of mercy. Keep track of your progress using the Table of Contents at the beginning of this book. Or you could make a poster of the corporal works of mercy and list the activities you have done that come under each one. Either a checklist or a poster can spur you on when you feel stuck in a rut.

Part III: Reflecting. While it is possible to perform acts of service as a family without any follow up, experts in the field of "service learning"—as well as those who make a vocation of serving others—say that service experiences bear the most fruit in people's lives when they have an opportunity to consciously and intentionally reflect on that experience. The final section of this book, Reflecting, is meant to help you integrate the activities and their meaning more fully into your family's faith life.

Sometimes, this may be as simple as a family discussion over dinner or talking about the service experience with a friend. In part III, however, I will share other ideas for making sure service learning doesn't stop when the activity ends.

Q: What are Peanut Butter & Grace and pbgrace.com?

Peanut Butter & Grace is a collection of resources aimed at helping parents raise their kids in the Catholic faith using practical family catechesis—that is, by practicing different dimensions of the faith with their kids. Peanut Butter & Grace books and online resources are designed to provide parents with a framework for living the Catholic faith with their kids in the setting of their family.

At pbgrace.com, you can look up additional resources for many of the sections in this book or leave comments about your own ideas and experiences. You'll find articles from the other books in the Peanut Butter & Grace series Guides for Catholic Families, as well as essays by Catholic parents and other great content. Plus, sign up for Family Time!, a weekly family faith formation newsletter.

Q: Who wrote this book?

I am first and foremost a parent- a parent who understands what it means to weed through life with the help of plenty of experts and sometimes few clear answers…a world where reality often falls short of our expectations. I am also an educator with a master's degree in instructional design and many years of experience teaching and directing in preschool and early-childhood settings. As an educator, I believe that raising confident, capable, faith-filled Catholic kids should be a joy-filled endeavor. Through my business, Work and Play Day by Day, I help moms transform their homeschool environment through family-centered resources and support. I am an author, speaker, teacher, and homeschooling mentor on a mission to make every parent an empowered parent. You can connect with me at www.workandplaydaybyday.com.

Q: Where did the ideas in this book come from?

Many of the ideas in this book have come from experiences with my family or from my time in classrooms working with children and families. Some activities we've completed and some we hope to do in the future. Other ideas come from friends, family, and community members with a shared passion for helping children learn to serve.

Q: Aren't you missing … ?

What about all those great activities that you've done that aren't included here? Yes, they're still great activities. But in my entire lifetime I could never list all the amazing opportunities to serve God with children. In selecting activities, I tried to consider each one in terms of its family friendliness. I gave priority to activities and organizations I think offer the best opportunities for children of all ages to learn, serve, and grow.

Q: What else can I do to nurture faith in my children?

In "Best Practices in Family Faith Formation," John Roberto identifies several recurring themes in the research literature on the faith lives of children and families. These themes point to five "core practices" that, "if consistently acted upon at home and supported by congregations, would contribute to building families of faithful Christians." Those practices are:

- having conversations that connect faith and daily life, and studying the faith together
- praying together, both at home and with the Church
- serving others together
- maintaining family rituals, traditions, and celebrations
- eating meals together

This book addresses the third of those core practices. Look for additional books in the Peanut Butter & Grace series **Guides for Catholic Families** to address the other core practices.

PART 1: PREPARING

Preparing, acting, and reflecting create a Cycle of Service. Preparing for your family service experience will help your family have a better—and more spiritually fruitful—experience.

In this part of the book, we will help you prepare for family service by going over the following topics:

- the nature of Christian service and the works of mercy
- strategies for overcoming barriers to family service
- preparing your kids for service by talking about some of the tough issues they might encounter
- ideas for building a culture of helping and service in your home

The Cycle of Service

A Crash Course in Christian Service

What Is Christian Service?

Service is, quite simply, caring for someone other than ourselves, often at some personal cost or sacrifice.

Jesus taught that caring for other people is a basic requirement of the kingdom of God. It is not "optional" or "extra" or "above and beyond" the normal duties of a follower of Jesus. In fact, in two parables, he taught that our eternal salvation depends on whether we served others with mercy and compassion, or turned away from those in need.

In the parable of the rich man and Lazarus (Luke 16:19–31), Jesus told the story of a rich man who ignores the needs of the poor beggar named Lazarus who lay at his doorstep. When the two men die, the rich man ends up in hell, while the poor man enjoys the comforts of heaven.

In the parable of the sheep and the goats (Matthew 25:34–40), Jesus says that those who served the needs of others (the "sheep") were really helping Christ in disguise, while those who ignored the needs of others ("the goats") were essentially ignoring the needs of Christ. The sheep are welcomed into heaven, while the goats are not.

The Works of Mercy

Because this parable of the judgment of the nations serves as the basis for the traditional listing of the corporal works of mercy, it would be valuable to take some time to read and reflect on it with your kids:

> "When the Son of Man comes in his glory, and all the angels with him, he will sit upon his glorious throne, and all the nations will be assembled before him. And he will separate them one from another, as a shepherd separates the sheep from the goats. He will place the sheep on his right and the goats on his left. Then the king will say to those on his right, 'Come, you who are blessed by my Father. Inherit the kingdom prepared for you from the foundation of the world. For I was hungry and you gave me food, I was thirsty and you gave me drink, a stranger and you welcomed me, naked and you clothed me, ill and you cared for me, in prison and you visited me.' Then the righteous will answer him and say, 'Lord, when did we see you hungry and feed you, or thirsty and give you drink? When did we see you a stranger and welcome you, or naked and clothe you? When did we see you ill or in prison, and visit you?' And the king

will say to them in reply, 'Amen, I say to you, whatever you did for one of these least brothers of mine, you did for me.' Then he will say to those on his left, 'Depart from me, you accursed, into the eternal fire prepared for the devil and his angels. For I was hungry and you gave me no food, I was thirsty and you gave me no drink, a stranger and you gave me no welcome, naked and you gave me no clothing, ill and in prison, and you did not care for me.' Then they will answer and say, 'Lord, when did we see you hungry or thirsty or a stranger or naked or ill or in prison, and not minister to your needs?' He will answer them, 'Amen, I say to you, what you did not do for one of these least ones, you did not do for me.' And these will go off to eternal punishment, but the righteous to eternal life." (Matthew 25:31–46)

The actions Jesus lists in this parable are drawn from the Old Testament tradition, especially Isaiah 58:6–11.

The parable was later developed into the traditional list of seven corporal (or bodily) works of mercy (see *Catechism*, #2447):

1. Feed the hungry
2. Give drink to the thirsty
3. Clothe the naked
4. Shelter the homeless
5. Visit the imprisoned
6. Visit the sick
7. Bury the dead

The seventh work of mercy, burying the dead, is taken from the book of Tobit. Much of the action of the story is launched by Tobit's insistence on providing a dignified burial to his Jewish neighbor, despite the threat of punishment for doing so. The seventh work of mercy recognizes that each person is more than just his or her body, but is actually the union of a body and a soul, destined for eternal life. God calls all people to himself, and it is this love of God that gives each and every person a dignity that we are called to respect and promote by providing for his or her basic bodily needs.

I have also included service ideas about care for our common home. This unofficial eighth corporal work of mercy comes from Pope Francis' encyclical on care for creation, *Laudato Si*, and other Church teachings.

"Let me propose a complement to the two traditional sets of seven [works of mercy]: may the works of mercy also include care for our common home. As a spiritual work of mercy, care for our common home calls for a "grateful contemplation of God's world" (*Laudato Si*, 214) which "allows us to discover in each thing a teaching which God wishes to hand on to us" (ibid., 85). As a corporal work of mercy, care for our common home requires "simple daily gestures which break with the logic of violence, exploitation and selfishness" and "makes itself felt in every action that seeks to build a better world" (ibid., 230–31). ("Message of Pope Francis for the Celebration of the World Day of Prayer for the Care of Creation," #5)

Pope Francis proposed that we see caring for the earth as a way to love God, Creator of this wondrous world, and the poor, who are most affected by damage to the earth. Your example can show your kids that the earth is to be nurtured, not exploited, and that its resources are given us as a gift from God, to use carefully and to share.

The works of mercy, and, in particular, care for the poor, have been part of the constant tradition of the Church. In fact, the *Catechism* of the Catholic Church addresses the works of mercy in its section about the seventh commandment, "You shall not steal." Quoting St. John Chrysostom, it goes so far as to say: "Not to enable the poor to share in our goods is to steal from them and deprive them of life. The goods we possess are not ours, but theirs" (*Catechism*, #2446).

> *"Remember that the Christian life is one of action; not of speech and daydreams. Let there be few words and many deeds, and let them be done well."*
>
> —St. Vincent Pallotti

A Christian Approach to Service

What makes Christian service particularly "Christian"? In other words, what makes it different from nonreligious service or activism? As you might conclude from the discussion above, Christian service is distinguished by reflection, prayer, and reliance on God. Most importantly, it is also characterized by faith. Christians (and other religious people) believe that when they serve others, they also serve God.

As Catholics, we can also look to Mary, the prototypical Christian, as we seek to model the attitudes of our own heart on hers. When she learned that her older relative Elizabeth was pregnant, Mary immediately journeyed by foot three days to care for her (Luke 1). Though she herself was expecting the Christ Child, she thought of pregnant Elizabeth's needs before her own. Mary thinks not of her own comfort, but of what is useful and what is needed. It is easy to imagine that this attitude marked her whole life, including the many years she spent serving the bodily needs of the child Jesus.

Addressing Barriers to Service

Let's acknowledge at the outset that barriers can make service difficult. They may be perceptual, practical, or even both. In this section, I address some common barriers and provide a few ideas for overcoming them. Throughout the book, I have included brief stories of saints that spotlight some of the brave and bold ways they served the poor, the sick, and the most vulnerable among society. Let their lives be a source of inspiration for you and your children. For more information, activities, and coloring pages for your children about these saints and many more, visit "Playing with the SAINTS!" and "Meet the Saints" at pbgrace.com.

"We don't have time for this."

Remember that (1) service is a faith-based activity, and (2) doing faith-based activities as a family is important. Family researcher Loren D. Marks notes two commonalities among families who regularly practice their faith together. First, these families set aside regular time for faith-based activities. Second, these families continue setting aside time for shared faith activities even when faced with objections from their children or when the activities go against popular culture (Rutledge, 2011). So we need to make time for family service.

In building a family culture of service, start small by integrating service into existing daily routines. For suggestions on teaching service from a very young age, see the many project and chore suggestions found in the sections "Building a Culture of Service at Home" (p. 37) and "Serving without Leaving Home" (p. 72).

> "If you have too much to do, with God's help you will find time to do it all."
>
> —St. Peter Canisius

You can also begin with some of the resources suggested in the section, "Talking about the Tough Stuff" (p. 25). Many of the children's books used for bedtime stories can lead to conversation, prayer, and action. After reading a book about homelessness, for example, add to your child's bedtime petitions a prayer for homeless children in your community and beyond. Over the next days, discuss homelessness in your community during family dinner or on car rides between activities. Then choose a project from this book (or ask your child to suggest their own) that can be done locally. Through these small additions to normal routines, you are making time for service.

Some families do an intentional service project on a regular basis, perhaps monthly or seasonally. Others make time to have regular, ongoing projects. Some choose to do activities mostly at home, while others prefer to interact with others in their community. Experiment with the ideas from this book, create your own and, whatever you do, don't stop if you feel your small contributions won't make a difference. There is no minimum or maximum when it comes to integrating service into your family routines. The Holy Spirit can work with whatever you have to offer!

"My kids are too little, or too far apart in age, for family service."

Service outside the home can seem overwhelming to parents of an infant or toddler. In truth, many infants and toddlers (and even younger preschoolers) are not yet ready for service outside the home, and that is just fine! Someday your child may be ready to visit a homeless shelter or organize their own garage sale for charity.

With younger children, you may naturally focus on the activities in the section "Building a Culture of Service at Home" (p. 37). These activities will build a foundation in your child's heart and a habit in your family that will pay off in the years to come.

On the other hand, some families rise to the challenge and successfully integrate young children—and even infants—into their family service activities. Professor of theology Susan Windley-Daoust recounts how her small children often did a better job than the adults at warmly welcoming the homeless and hungry people at a local shelter. Even her infant son became an instrument of grace when a homeless man was allowed to cradle him. "I never thought that at age six months, my son would be doing the works of mercy more effectively than anyone else in the family," she says ("Motherhood, Hospitality, and the Catholic Worker: Vocations that Heal" at pbgrace.com/).

"Everyone has the power for greatness, not for fame but greatness, because greatness is determined by service."

—Martin Luther King, Jr.

When working with a mixed-age group of children, provide a variety of activities or combine activities to create a full family experience. I've included in this book activities for a wide range of ages, avoiding those unsuitable for young children, unless noted otherwise. You can adapt or combine most of them to include all members of the family in some way.

For example, in serving at a funeral, the younger children can color place mats for the meal, the middle school-aged children can make a salad or dessert, and the teenagers can serve the meal or assist at the Mass. Before or after attending a funeral as a family, tie the experience together using the resources and discussion questions regarding death and dying found in the section "Talking about the Tough Stuff" (p. 25).

And no matter what kind of service you do with your kids, bringing it back into prayer and conversation can point all of you toward love of God through love of others.

"We don't have money for extras as it is."

A friend pointed out to me, upon reading a draft of this manuscript, that her experience growing up was much different than mine. In her parish, stewardship always seemed like a code for "we need money." She noted that in every parish she has observed, a few people are the doers of projects and most others prefer giving financially to help.

We can't overlook the need for money in some service projects. In fact, many of the projects in this text contain opportunities to creatively provide financial support for them. Try, though, to think of stewardship not as an either/or, but rather as a both/and. Needs in our communities require both money and actions. At times we do better at contributing actions, other times we do better at financial support. There is a balance, and it is up to each family to find their own.

In this book, I have indicated activities requiring little or no money by placing a "$" next to them. If your family is not able to spend money to serve others at this time, don't worry that you won't be able to help. You can bless others by using what you already have and by being who you are.

"I don't have the knowledge or skills to help someone else."

Remember that family service involves a cycle of preparing, acting, and reflecting. Your family does not need specific knowledge or skills to begin serving someone. In fact, gaining that knowledge or skill is its own step in preparing for service. When you observe the needs of a community, group, or person you want to serve, you are also assessing whether you have the skills to meet that need. Perhaps you can gain a new skill or expand your knowledge through conversation about one of the corporal works of mercy, as suggested in "Talking about the Tough Stuff" (p. 25).

You may conclude that a specific activity is not right for your family right now, and that is OK. You have then learned something that might help you identify a person who is right for the job. You may be the "eyes and ears" of the body of Christ this week, instead of the "hands and feet."

Still unsure of what you can do? Start by identifying what is already happening around you. What does your church do? Consider committing in some small way to at least one opportunity to serve announced at church. Even if you participate alone instead of with your family, you will serve others, set an example for your children, and begin to discover the activities for which your family may be particularly well suited.

"I am afraid to take my kids into that environment."

We live in a crazy and sometimes scary world. I would be the last person to tell you that you should serve anyone, anywhere, at any time with no regard for the safety and needs of your own family. That being said, unexamined fear is not a good reason to avoid serving.

If your concern is safety at an activity, you can speak with the coordinators of an event or organization and perhaps make a visit to the site alone prior to bringing your children. Your concern might be the location of the volunteer site, the type of work involved, or the people being served. If your concern is warranted, you might support the activity from a different location, such as helping to stuff envelopes or organizing materials in advance. In this text, you will notice that I have not included many opportunities directly related to visiting the imprisoned. Prisons and other such institutions have age limits for volunteering, and serving there may not fit your family. In the "Talking about the Tough Stuff" section, however, I have included a few ideas for how your family can still serve prisoners (p. 25).

"One of the clearest service memories I have from childhood is singing at a local nursing home every month. Though I felt awkward around elderly and ill people when I was younger, I now appreciate the experience of getting to know nursing home residents as people."

Are you concerned about personal discomfort? Well, the only way to move past that is simply to put yourself out there. Educating yourself and your family about the specific place you'd like to visit can go a long way toward easing the discomfort of a new situation. If you need to, take small steps and start with activities you can participate in from a distance and work toward more direct involvement. After an activity, allow your family to share with one another their experiences of the event openly and honestly. Remind your children and yourself that most of us grow into things gradually through practice.

Talking about the Tough Stuff

Service often brings us face-to-face with difficult circumstances and tough issues. That's one of the benefits of serving others: Service takes us out of our comfort zone, expands our horizons, and helps us develop empathy for others. Still, some of these topics are tough even for adults to process, and more so kids. For the best possible family service experience, you'll want to prepare your children for the tough stuff that might come up during the activity. The sections below give some background on what you might encounter when doing the works of mercy and address some situations that might arise.

When speaking with your children about a hard situation, be sure to listen to their concerns and do your best to relieve any fears they may have. Young children, in particular, will often be scared that such things might happen to them (e.g., homelessness, serious illness, death or loss of someone dear, lack of food). Though we might want to promise them that this sort of thing will never happen to our family, realistically, it could. Reassure your child with lots of love and any practical information that you can. Regarding homelessness, for example, is there somewhere you know you could live (with a relative perhaps) if you were forced out of your home for any reason? Talk about local organizations that help families who find themselves homeless due to natural disaster or fire. Particularly with younger children, don't overwhelm them with too many details. Watch your children for cues of what kind or level of information they need, and remember to balance it with lots of hugs, snuggles, and love!

Older children and teenagers may reach a point in their development when they want to know more about what the Catholic Church teaches on many of these tough issues, and why. You can start looking for answers at the website of the U.S. Conference of Catholic Bishops, or the Compendium of the Social Doctrine of the Church. For more information on this topic, see "Five Ways to Help Catholic Kids Talk about Church Teaching on Tough Issues" at pbgrace.com. Additional resources on Catholic social teaching are also available in Part III (p. 78).

How to Use This Section

The following sections are designed to be used on an as-needed basis. You may choose to use them as an outline for family catechesis and study, focusing on one area at a time. You may start with one topic that is interesting to your family and then choose an activity from part II that suggests practical ways to apply what you have discussed. Or, you may choose an activity first and then prepare for that activity by discussing the underlying work of mercy involved.

No matter how you use the following section, it is meant to be a starting point for family discussion. You may need to go deeper, or you may not use all of the resources provided. In no way do you need to cover every topic, resource, and discussion question before diving into your first service activity. You have my full permission to take what works for your family and leave the rest. Simply bookmark the start of this section to return when you are ready for the next topic.

Sheltering the Homeless

"Do not neglect hospitality, for through it some have unknowingly entertained angels." (Hebrews 13:2)

This passage from Hebrews refers to the story of Abraham providing hospitality to three travelers who turned out to be angels, messengers of God (Genesis 18). In biblical times, welcoming a stranger into one's home was especially important because travelers often didn't have another place to stay.

Today we welcome strangers when we advocate for those who are migrants or refugees from other countries. The Bible mentions aid to alien (non-native) residents more than one hundred times, and most of those references command the Israelites to treat foreigners with compassion. "You shall treat the alien who resides with you no differently than the natives born among you; you shall love the alien as yourself; for you too were once aliens in the land of Egypt. I, the Lord, am your God" (Leviticus 19:34).

We know, of course, that besides migrants and refugees, many other people—families as well as individuals—are without a home. Possibly your child knows someone from school or church who, unbeknown to your child, is homeless or living in material poverty. Homelessness can result from many circumstances, not all of them directly related to poverty. You have probably heard it said that many families are just a paycheck, a car repair, or an illness away from homelessness.

In 2010 a major house fire left us without a place to live. Even with insurance, it took a lot of time and resources to relocate us to a temporary home, and more than six months for our house to be livable. In the meantime, we were shuttled between hotels courtesy of the Red Cross and offered hospitality in the homes of friends and family. At times, we were located outside the boundaries of our local school district and far from my husband's employment. Getting to jobs and schools is one of the main challenges for the chronically homeless.

In your area, your family may find places you can visit to serve those who don't have a home to call their own. Spending time with homeless children (and foster children, who do not have a permanent home) can help your young ones understand that these children are like them in so many ways. They like to play with dolls and cars and blocks. They like to swing and climb and run and jump.

Family Discussion Questions on Homelessness

- What are some of the reasons a family might be without a home?
- What do you think would be the hardest part about not having a home?
- What are some ways that families without a home are the same as families with a home? What are some ways they might be different?

Children's Literature for Talking about Homelessness

Carlson, Natalie Savage. *The Family Under the Bridge.* **Harper Collins, 1989.** The story of an unlikely family formed by a homeless man and a group of homeless children living under a bridge in Paris. A Newberry Honor Book.

Martin, Chia. *Rosie: The Shopping Cart Lady.* **Hohm Press, 1996.** A rhyming story of the help a young boy provides to a woman on the street after she is injured.

McGovern, Ann. *The Lady in the Box.* **Turtle Books, 1999.** Two young children befriend a homeless woman living on their street in New York City.

Trottier, Maxine. *A Safe Place.* **Albert Whitman & Co., 1997.** A young girl and her mother move into a shelter for battered women.

Visiting the Imprisoned

"I was … in prison and you visited me." (Matthew 25:35–36)

Most prisoners in the U.S. are incarcerated due to criminal activity. But some people around the world are imprisoned for reasons that are not criminal. Some are prisoners of war; some have been imprisoned because of religious or political beliefs; and some have been kidnapped for child labor or sexual slavery. Refugees living in resettlement camps may experience imprisonment to the extent that they cannot return home, and they are unable to leave the camp. Even girls who are restricted from attending school experience a type of imprisonment.

Obviously, the ability to discuss each of these issues will depend on the maturity of the child involved. Certainly you wouldn't talk about women being kidnapped to serve as sex slaves with a preschooler or other young child, but it may be very appropriate with a high schooler or college-aged young person.

For all children, the struggles of prisoners, criminal or otherwise, are difficult to think about. That being said, children have an incredible capacity for empathy. With proper support, they can respond well to meeting and interacting with almost any new person. Responding to imprisonment, possibly more than any other of the tough issues we deal with here, demands an ever-growing understanding of the complex issues facing those involved. Family conversations can help.

Working directly with those who have been imprisoned would be extremely difficult for families and, as such, I do not recommend taking it on lightly. If your family feels called to this ministry, a local prison ministry through your diocesan Catholic Charities may be able to point you to opportunities for service in your area. To serve this population, you can also use the knowledge you gain through resources and family discussion to engage in political action by writing a letter to the editor or corresponding with a politician (p. 73). Older teens and adults in the family may help in local programs that support those who are reintegrating into society following imprisonment. To include younger members of your family, consider putting together and sending a care package (p. 74).

Family Discussion Questions about Imprisonment

- What does it mean to be imprisoned?
- What are some ways and reasons that someone could be imprisoned?
- What are some ways that imprisonment affects families?
- How can we help the families of those who are imprisoned?
- As a family, look through a newspaper or news magazine for all the examples and references to imprisonment you can find, and discuss these.

Resources for Talking about Imprisonment

Ernst, Kathleen. *Caroline's Secret Message*. American Girl Publishing, 2012. In this historical fiction story, Caroline's father is taken as a prisoner of war.

Sesame Street Workshop. "Little Children, Big Challenges: Incarceration,"

in the parents' topics and activities section of sesamestreet.org. This on-line resource includes videos and other resources for talking with a child about their own parent's incarceration. You might preview these resources before using them to discuss issues of imprisonment with your own children.

Visiting the Sick

"Simon's mother-in-law lay sick with a fever. They immediately told him about here. He approached, grasped her hand, and helped her up. Then the fever left her and she waited on them." (Mark 1:30–31)

Historically, religious organizations have been a primary source of health care. Christians were often the only ones to care for the sick during plagues. The martyrs of Alexandria, Egypt, in the third century famously stayed in the city to care for the dying after the rest of the population had fled. Later, religious orders founded hospitals to care for the sick and dying.

Chances are, you do not have to go outside your friends and family to know someone with a chronic or life-limiting illness—someone homebound, in a nursing home, or with a serious physical or mental disability. Possibly your child's questions about such people have already prompted discussions on this topic.

Alzheimer's disease can be particularly confining, as an otherwise healthy adult becomes unable to remember how to do many simple tasks, even forgetting the names and faces of their closest friends and family. Children and adults with autism face the overwhelming sights and sounds of a busy street, grocery store, or church and may struggle to participate in society. You may want to talk about severe or terminal illness as feeling like a kind of imprisonment, especially if affected persons are confined to one place—whether a hospital, a nursing home, or even their home. A child in a wheelchair my feel like a prisoner to their disability if they are unable to fully participate on the playground or on a school field trip due to inaccessibility.

Family Discussion Questions about Illness

- What does it feel like to be sick and not able to visit with friends or do the things that you like to do?
- hat is a chronic illness?
- What would each family member miss the most if they were sick for a long period of time?

- Do you know anyone with Alzheimer's disease? What is their life like? Their family's life?

- What are some ways our family can be a friend to a person with a physical or mental disability?

Children's Literature for Talking about Illness

Schnurbush, Barbara. *Striped Shirts and Flowered Pants: A Story About Alzheimer's Disease for Young Children*. Magination Press, 2007. This story follows a young girl as she learns to understand her grandmother's illness; a family discussion guide included.

Buckley, Colleen. *Grandma Kathy Has Cancer*. Dog Ear Publishing, 2007. As a young girl interacts with her grandmother who has cancer, she learns about the many ups and downs of living with cancer.

Peterkin, Allan. *What About Me?* Magination Press, 1992. Written for siblings of a child facing extended illness and hospitalization, this book addresses feelings of exclusion and loneliness, along with uncertainty and misunderstanding of the illness.

Shriver, Maria. *What's Wrong with Timmy?* Little Brown Books for Young Readers, 2001. A little girl named Kate meets a boy named Timmy with Down Syndrome. Discusses being a friend to a person with a disability. While aimed at Down Syndrome specifically, this is a good book to use as a springboard for a discussion about relating to youth and adults with different abilities.

Feeding the Hungry, Giving Drink to the Thirsty

"And whoever gives only a cup of cold water to one of these little ones to drink because he is a disciple—amen, I say to you, he will surely not lose his reward." (Matthew 10:42)

When you're thirsty, you can probably head to the kitchen for a drink of water. Explain to your children that in Jesus' time, it was not so simple. To get water, you had to walk to the nearest source, which was probably a well or cistern, draw out the water by hand one bucket at a time, and then carry it back.

Unfortunately, nearly a billion people around the world face a similar situation today. Many of those people are women and girls who spend hours each day walking to the nearest source of water and carrying it home on their backs or heads—using time and energy that may keep them from school or other work. Often, that water is not even clean. Water-borne diseases kill 3.4 million people a year, mostly children. Another 2.5 billion people lack access to adequate sanitation.

Hunger also continues to affect many families even today. About three million people die of hunger or malnutrition every year, according to one study. Even in the U.S., some forty-nine million Americans (including sixteen million children) live in food-insecure households. Food insecure means that families often run out of food and skip meals as a result. Kids who don't get enough to eat do poorly in school and may develop lifelong health problems.

Incredibly, most of these people aren't hungry because of food shortages. In the United States alone, one third of all edible food—about 133 billion pounds—gets thrown away. Growers throw away produce that is blemished or misshapen, even if it is edible, because consumers won't buy produce that doesn't look perfect. Grocery stores overstock their perishable items so they won't run out, and end up unnecessarily throwing away a lot of it. Consumers buy more food than they can use and put more than they can (or should) eat on their plates.

Hunger and thirst may be the easiest of the tough topics in this book for our children to relate to. They know what it feels like when their stomachs have gone a bit too long between meals, what it feels like to wake up hungry in the morning, or to be thirsty after playing hard. They have a context for hunger and thirst, even if they don't fully understand what it means to face those struggles every day on the same scale that so many around the world do. This can make for fruitful conversations with even younger children, and they may feel drawn to act.

Family Discussion Questions about Hunger and Thirst

- How can fasting during certain seasons of the liturgical year help us develop a better understanding of hunger?
- How many restaurants and fast-food places are located between your home and church or school? Do restaurants help or hurt the battle against hunger?
- How much food do we throw away every day?
- How much water do we use each day? How would life be different if we didn't have access to unlimited clean water?

Children's Literature for Talking about Hunger and Thirst

Kerley, Barbara. *A Cool Drink of Water*. National Geographic Children's Books, 2002. A picture book of people around the world and the many ways they gather, transport, and drink water.

McBrier, Page. *Beatrice's Goat*. Atheneum Books for Young Readers, 2001. The story of what happens when someone sponsors a family to receive a goat from an organization such as Heifer Project International (HPI). With the sale of milk and baby goats, Beatrice is able to attend school for the first time. Two percent of profits from this book are donated to HPI.

Disalvo-Ryan, Dyanne. *Uncle Willie and the Soup Kitchen*. Morrow Junior Books, 1991. Uncle Willie works in a soup kitchen, and one day he brings his nephew to work with him. The boy discovers the spirit of community and giving in each of the people who visits the kitchen for work or for food.

Milway, Katie Smith. *The Good Garden: How One Family Went from Hunger to Having Enough*. Kids Can Press, 2010. The fictionalized story of Don Elias Sanchez, who taught families from small villages farming techniques to allow them to achieve food independence. See also thegoodgarden.org.

Clothing the Naked

"I spread the corner of my cloak over you to cover your nakedness."
(Ezekiel 16:8)

Many saints were known for their generosity with the poor. They became particularly zealous in their giving when they discovered that freeing themselves from material attachments gave them more joy than they ever got from their possessions. Antony of Egypt, an early pioneer of monasticism, gave away all he had to the poor and lived in the desert, and devoted his life to prayer and fasting. As a family, you could research one of these other saints known for their charitable works and simple living: Francis of Assisi, Queen Margaret of Scotland, or Queen Elizabeth of Hungary.

Growing up, I remember a girl in my class who lived with her grandma. She had to wear each outfit for two days before being allowed to wear another, and she rotated between only two or three. When we were younger, no one seemed to notice, but by the end of elementary school, other children were making comments about her, and she began to face isolation due to her family's circumstances. Most of us took clean and appropriate clothing for granted, but this child did not have that luxury.

As parents, we might worry about how expensive back-to-school shopping will be when our children's jeans shrink six inches (or more!) over the summer, but we know we will most likely be able to make it work. In most parts of the U.S., we have access to hand-me-downs, garage sales, thrift stores, back-to-school sales, and more. Our children probably won't be kept from school or activities because they don't have appropriate shoes or clothing. Yet many children around the world have that exact problem. Some adults are kept from interviewing for jobs that could help them overcome poverty because they lack clean or appropriate clothing for the job.

Family Discussion Questions about Clothing the Naked

- How many days could each person in your family go without washing clothes?
- If you had to select just one or two play outfits and one dress outfit for special occasions, what would you select? If you had to select only one pair of shoes, which would you choose?
- How can we care for our clothing in the best ways so that we'll be able to share with others and conserve resources?

Children's Literature for Talking about Clothing the Naked

Taback, Timms. *Joseph Had a Little Overcoat*. Viking Books for Young Readers, 1999. Just because an item is worn out or no longer fits doesn't mean that it can't still be useful. This book helps younger children to understand the many ways we can reuse an item even if it is old and worn. A Caldecott Medal Book.

Ajmera, Maya. *What We Wear: Dressing Up Around the World*. Charlesbridge, 2012. A global look at what children around the world wear to school, worship, play, and more. Includes family activities for discussing cultural variations in clothing.

Judge, Lita. *One Thousand Tracings*. Disney-Hyperion, 2007. In the aftermath of World War II, a farm family helps their German friends recover by collecting shoes and clothing from their home and from their friends. Before long, thousands of tracings of feet are showing up in their mailbox from other families who also need help.

Williams, Karen Lynn, and Khadra Mohammed. *Four Feet, Two Sandals*. Eerdmans, 2016. The story of the friendship forged in a refugee camp between two girls sharing one pair of shoes.

Burying the Dead

"He went to Pilate and asked for the body of Jesus. After he had taken the body down, he wrapped it in a linen cloth and laid him in a rock-hewn tomb in which no one had yet been buried." (Luke 23:52–53)

The book of Tobit describes how Tobit, an upstanding Jew, risked properly burying a dead man—even though he might have been exiled for it. The story underlines the importance that Jews, Christians, and most people around the world place on burying the dead reverently. This is why the action of Joseph of Arimathea in the passage quoted above serves as a model for all Christians.

It might seem strange that burying the dead would be among the works of mercy. The dead don't appear to benefit from our acts of charity the way a thirsty or hungry person might. But consider this passage from the Church's Order of Christian Funerals:

At the death of a Christian, whose life of faith was begun in the waters of Baptism and strengthened at the Eucharistic table, the Church intercedes on behalf of the deceased because of its confident belief that death is not the end, nor does it break the bonds forged in life. The Church also ministers to the sorrowing and consoles them in the funeral rites with the comforting Word of God and the Sacrament of the Eucharist. (Order of Christian Funerals, #4)

The Church's rituals for burying the dead serve several purposes. First, the funeral Mass and other prayers for the dead are a way of interceding for them. The practice of praying for the dead dates back at least as far as a couple centuries before Christ (2 Maccabees 12:38–45) and has long been part of the Christian tradition. The Church teaches that the souls of those who die in friendship with God but who are not completely purified of sin are assured eternal salvation, but must first undergo a final purification from sin ("purgatory") in order to enter the joy of heaven (*Catechism* of the Catholic Church, #1030–31). We pray for the dead to help them with this purification, to remember them, and to honor them. After all, as Christians we believe that death does not sever our relationship with friends and relatives, but only changes it.

Second, the funeral Mass is a celebration of the person's life—not just his life on earth, but also his new life in Christ. Even though it is perfectly natural to be sad when someone dies, Christians can be confident that they are not saying goodbye to their loved ones forever.

Third, the funeral rites, especially the Eucharist, the reading of the Word of God, and the prayers, help comfort those who have lost someone they love.

My own children have had plenty of experience with this work of mercy. They have buried two sisters: one who passed away in utero in my third trimester and one with severe congenital deformities who lived for only a couple of hours. I have also had three miscarriages; though we didn't hold funerals or burials in those cases, our children are aware of them. As much as I would have wished to spare my children from this heartache, these life realities have shown me their most compassionate side. I am now convinced that parents often put off the topic of death for far too long with their children. When I finally worked up the courage to tell my five-year-old about a miscarriage, she gave me a big joyful hug and said, "Don't worry, Mommy! The angels came and took our baby straight to Heaven!"

Death is scary and sad, but exposing children to this reality through conversation and service will better prepare them for that inevitable time when it hits closer to home. Service opportunities give them a chance to experience the respect and dignity that we can show in life's final journey. I, for one, have always been grateful for the Catholic teachings on death and dying that give us so much reason to hope.

Family Discussion Questions about Burying the Dead

- What is a funeral Mass? Share experiences with those who have never attended. If applicable, share experiences with other types of Christian and non-Christian burial services.

- Why is it important to participate in funeral Masses?

- Why do we visit cemeteries and pray for the dead? (*Catechism* of the Catholic Church, #1030–32.)

Resources for Talking about Death and Dying

Stickney, Doris. *Water Bugs and Dragonflies: Explaining Death to Young Children.* **Pilgrim Press, 1997.** A simple story of the transition from water bug to dragonfly. The water bugs make a promise to come back and tell the other water bugs what life is like above the pond, but once transformed the dragonfly tries, but realizes he can't go back. Includes notes about talking with children about death.

DePaola, Tomie. *Nana Upstairs and Nana Downstairs.* **Puffin Books, 2000.** Based on his own childhood experiences of visiting his grandma and great grandma each week, Tomie dePaola shares his perspective on their aging and death.

Prenatal Partners for Life. *Our Baby Died and Went to Heaven.* **2009.** A brief illustrated book, interspersed with Scripture, to provide comfort and understanding to a child following the death of a baby. Available from prenatalpartnersforlife.org.

Curley, Terence P. *Six Steps for Managing Loss: A Catholic Guide through Grief.* **Alba House, 1997.** Full of insights, reflection, and guided prayers, this book by a Catholic priest helps the reader cope with grief through the lens of a Catholic understanding of death, including developing a spiritual relationship with the deceased. Written for adults.

Building a Culture of Service at Home

The family is the primary setting for socialization, since it is where we first learn to relate to others, to listen and share, to be patient and show respect, to help one another and live as one. The task of education is to make us sense that the world and society are also our home; it trains us how to live together in this greater home. In the family, we learn closeness, care and respect for others. We break out of our fatal self-absorption and come to realize that we are living with and alongside others who are worthy of our concern, our kindness and our affection. (Pope Francis, *Amoris Laetitia*, #276)

Loving and serving one another is (ideally) what families do. The family is where children learn what the works of mercy look and feel like. A mother nursing her child is feeding the hungry. A father carrying his tired or injured child home from the park is caring for the sick. A brother who makes a snack for his sister while mom is sick in bed is doing both. We can spend all day in acts of service without ever leaving the front door of our home. Indeed, most service does and should begin in the home.

So I include in part I on preparing some ideas for how to build a culture of helping and service at home, which is the best preparation for doing the works of mercy in the wider world.

Care for Siblings

Don't be shy about recruiting older siblings to help younger children—and when you do, make an explicit link to the works of mercy. Think about how many opportunities there are to "clothe the naked" when you have a toddler!

Younger children can find ways to serve older kids, too. From a young age, encourage children to contribute to the well-being of the other members of their family. To intimately know the person receiving help and to see the immediate impact of their own actions creates a deep understanding in children that serving others is important and worthwhile.

Buddy System

Implement a "buddy system" in your family, recruiting older children to train younger children in the rhythms and routines of the family.

- It is especially helpful for a designated older sibling to help their younger "buddy" during transition times, assisting with young ones' shoes and coats when the family is trying to get out of the house, or holding hands in the parking lot.

- Point out how the older children's helpful ways not only serve their siblings but also help you as a parent. They are building skills they may someday need in their own life vocations.

Royalty for the Day

One of our favorite family-based service activities is to make one person "royalty" for the day.

- On someone's birthday or another special day (e.g., baptism anniversary, patron saint's feast day, etc.), everyone else will look for as many ways as possible to serve the special person. It is really fun to see how creative the other children can be: making special meals or favorite foods, playing games they don't like, helping with their chores, and more.

- Royalty for the day is not limited to kids; adults can be royalty, too.

Chores

Learning to do household chores might seem inconsequential in light of the world's many problems, but our faith teaches that, far from being trivial, our daily work can be a means to holiness. Numerous Catholic saints—Brother Lawrence, Thérèse of Lisieux, and Martin de Porres, to name a few—have developed a spirituality that emphasizes the importance of doing even menial chores with great love in the service of God.

It can be tempting to assume that our children will figure out how to be helpful on their own. A related pitfall is to assume that our kids ought to see the messes around the house the way we do—and then respond with the responsibility of an adult. "Can't you see the counter is a mess? Why didn't you wipe it down?" But the reality is that forming any new habit requires learning, time, and self-discipline. (I sometimes think of self-discipline as choosing to be more stubborn than my natural inclinations!) In other words, the habits and skills related to being helpful around the house don't come naturally; they need to be taught. Guess who gets to be their teacher!

It is true that teaching kids how to do household chores is initially way more work than just doing them yourself. It's also true that your kids will rarely do a chore as well as you might, at least in the beginning. But besides boosting your kids' character, if you stick with it, in time you'll be rewarded with extra capable and helpful kids and teens who are able to pitch in

Examples of Chores by Age

Area of home	Ages 3–6	Ages 7–12	Ages 13+
Bedrooms	Make bed Put away toys	Vacuum Dust	Independent care of bedroom
Kitchen/meals	Set table Clear table after meals Help with simple meal prep tasks Hand wash some dishes	Put away groceries Assist with meal preparation Empty and load dishwasher Clean counters Hand wash dishes	Prepare meals independently Clean oven Clean out refrigerator, cabinets
Pet care	Give food and water Simple animal training	Learn to handle a small pet independently Change bedding or litter, clean yard	Take dog on longer walks Groom and monitor pet's health
Outside work	Help plant and harvest garden Pick up yard Rake leaves Sweep porches and sidewalks	Weed Shovel snow Clean out and wash car	Mow grass Trim edges and bushes Car and household maintenance
Bathrooms	Empty trash cans Wash mirrors with vinegar/water and old t-shirt	Scrub toilets Sweep and mop Refill soap dispenser	Clean tub and sinks Scrub floor
Common areas	Dust Pick up toys Straighten shelves	Sweep Take out garbage and recycling	Mop Clean windows
Clothing	Bring dirty laundry to hamper Sort colors Fold towels Match socks	Run the washer and dryer Fold all clothes Put away own clothes	Hang clothes outside Iron Responsibility for own laundry

around the house more independently, meaning less work for you down the road. Besides, having household chores taken care of quickly and efficiently will free up more time for all the other great service activities in this book!

Here, then, are some tips for teaching kids to do chores around the home:

- **Emphasize an attitude of helpfulness.** Emphasize an attitude of helpfulness rather than duty. For example, saying, "I really could use your help!" and "Thanks so much—you were a big help!" brings a positive dimension to chores by highlighting the basic human desire to help others and contribute to the well-being of the group. "You'll clean your room because I told you to," by contrast, may be effective in the short run, but frames the work in terms of a power struggle.

- **Start young.** As much as possible, keep toddlers close by as you work, and give them chore-related tools to play with (e.g., an extra rag, the dustpan, etc.). (And yes, "toddler" and "getting things done" don't usually go together. It might be helpful to think of these times less in terms of getting things done and more in terms of ten or fifteen minutes of "chore school" for your little one.) Children are most ready to learn about work around the home by age three. Often, preschoolers will be your most enthusiastic helpers—strike while the iron is hot!

- **It's all about expectations.** Whining, complaining, and passive resistance often discourage parents from expecting their kids to help around the house. But here's something to keep in mind: kids are all about expectations. Start teaching them to be helpful and responsible from an early age, and you will encounter much less resistance down the road because helping around the house will be "normal." Does that mean you can't teach older kids to help around the house, or raise expectations for how much they help? Not at all. Older children may initially balk at your efforts to raise the chore standards, but stick with it until they adapt. The older your child is, the longer this may take; you just need to be more stubborn (self-disciplined!) than your child.

- **Work side by side with your child.** While some jobs are appropriate for children to do independently, most require a period of direct learning. Work side by side with your child, particularly in the beginning, and check in regularly to improve your child's attitude toward the chore and their skill at it. Young children can do quite a lot when we take the time to teach them.

- **Pitch in on big jobs.** Kids are easily overwhelmed and discouraged when we give them big jobs—a whole lawn to rake, or a whole room to clean up. Depending on their age and experience, it can be difficult for kids to break down a big job into smaller tasks. Working alongside them the first few times (or until they're old enough) can be hugely helpful. Don't think of it as letting them off the hook—think of it as teaching them persistence, and how to break a big job down into smaller, more manageable pieces.

- **Practice noticing.** Practice the art of noticing with your children to train them to identify the needs of the spaces around them. Notice when things are done well and point out how relaxing it feels to enjoy orderly spaces. At our house, we play a clean-up game based on "I Spy." I stand in the middle of the room and "spy" things that are out of place while the kids race to fix them. When my older kids are transitioning to independence in cleaning tasks, I challenge them to play the noticing game before I check off their work area. If they can notice the needs of spaces, it begins to translate into noticing the needs of people. In fact, we call this the noticing game.

- **Experiment with chore charts.** Some families use chore charts to keep track of who is responsible for what around the house. A chore chart can be as simple or complex as you like; Pinterest is an excellent source of ideas. Just remember that chore charts are a tool to help your family stay organized, on task, and motivated. As such, your chore chart will probably need to change over time. If you find yourself not using your chore chart after a while, don't feel guilty—it may be a sign that your situation has changed. It might be that you need to come up with a new chore chart, or it might be that a chart isn't what you need anymore.

- **Keep your expectations developmentally appropriate.** What kids can do around the house will change as their cognitive and motor skills develop and mature. Expecting young kids to perform tasks that their minds and bodies aren't equipped for will just result in frustration. Above (on p. 39), you will find a basic table listing age-appropriate chore expectations. Adjust these suggestions based on the age and maturity of your child, or even the size of the space.

In all things, do what works for your family, keeping in mind that what works in one season of your family life might not work in another.

PART II: ACTING

The next step in the Cycle of Service is acting. This is the moment when our Christian faith becomes more than just words and holy sentiments; like Christ, we enter the world "to bring glad tidings to the poor … to proclaim liberty to captives and recovery of sight to the blind, to let the oppressed go free …" (Luke 4:18).

In this part of the book, I offer some ideas for action. The ideas broken down into the traditional works of mercy, plus the new work of mercy proposed by Pope Francis: care for creation. The last part includes service projects to get your family started without having to leave the home. Many of these ideas build service skills and mark by integrating service at home.

Feed the Hungry, Give Drink to the Thirsty, Clothe the Naked

Feeding the hungry, giving drink to the thirsty, and clothing the naked all fall under the umbrella of caring for our neighbors immediate bodily needs. Often our work in these areas involves the donation of physical goods.

Sometimes the hardest part of donating is finding the right organization to connect with and learning what types of donations are useful and most needed. One of the churches where I taught had a list in the kitchen of local places that would accept leftovers on behalf of those in need in the community. If we had leftovers after a school event, we knew exactly where they could go in order to minimize waste. Reach out to your church, your community, and your friends. Our neighbors' needs do not stop at hunger and thirst. And the talents and skills your family has to share with others can fill a material or educational void and immediate need.

Make a blessing box (3+, 7+, 13+)

People in times of crisis or less-fortunate situations might be desperate for things other than food. Their children might need school supplies, baby supplies, and books. People can be hungry and thirsty for many physical needs. To fill that need in your community, considering making a blessing box with your family. Older children and parents can help build the box, and younger children can paint and decorate the box. The box is placed, with permission, at a church or local library, for example. Elementary school children can help write letters to churches and libraries to find a good home for the box.

Now, as a family, fill the box with needed items: groceries, books, toothbrushes, water bottles, soap, and diapers. People in the community are encouraged to continue to fill the box as it empties. Although it doesn't take the place of an established food pantry, it can make a difference in filling an immediate and desperate need, as well as instill an attitude of service for your entire family. Find out more at pbgrace.com/blessing-boxes.

Plant an extra row (3+, 7+, 13+)

If your family plants a garden, you may be interested to know that many food shelves accept donations of fresh-from-the-garden produce in addition to non-perishables. Donations are often down in the summer. Consider planting an extra row of vegetables so you can donate your bounty. Soup kitchens and other meal services will also take donations of produce, with quantity guidelines. Keep track of the pounds of garden produce you donate and then see if you can beat it the next year!

Make a meal for a family with a new baby or for a family in crisis (7+, 13+)

It's true that every child is a gift from God, but it's also true that adding a new baby to the family can also be stressful and tiring for everyone (especially Mom!). When you hear about a family that has a new arrival, get your kids involved in making a meal (or even a special snack or care package) and drop it off the family. And remember that such meals are usually just as welcome several weeks or months after the baby is born—many babies are the most work when they are two to four months old. If you're good friends with the family, consider organizing a meal train among the family's friends and neighbors. Many online services now make it a snap to coordinate meals among a large group.

Similarly, families go through times of crisis and struggle. Maybe a family member has died, or a child is in the NICU or hospital for an extended period of time. These are times of stress and having one less thing to do (like figuring out what to make for dinner) is a blessing.

If you cannot make a meal, for whatever reason, gifting a family with an online supermarket gift card can be incredibly helpful and practical. Send the gift card in a personalized, homemade card from your younger children.

Serve at a soup kitchen, community meal, food shelf, or donation center ($, 7+, 13+)

This might seem obvious, but don't overlook the great service of a soup kitchen. If your community is home to a soup kitchen, volunteer to serve at one of their meals. In some communities, church congregations rotate the hosting of community meals. Some organizations have age limits, so call before you go and make sure they have jobs for everyone in your family who will be coming. Food shelves rely almost exclusively on volunteers to organize donations and distribute them onto the shelves. Call ahead before you bring a donation, ask for a tour to learn more about the way it is organized, and volunteer to help shelve your items and other donations that arrive that day.

Organize a food drive (3+, 7+, 13+)

Community food banks have peak seasons and temporary shortages. Call your local food bank and find out what they need most. You could organize a drive to fill the shelves at the food bank. You can pass out flyers in your neighborhood or request that an announcement be placed in your parish bulletin with the specific need. This is a great activity for a service club you might start (p. 90). Have younger children help organize donations, and encourage older ones to create and distribute flyers.

"I brought my nine-year-old son with me to the St. Vincent de Paul Soup Kitchen. He wasn't old enough to work on the food line, but they had him work in the corner rolling silverware packets. He was talking to everyone while he worked, and I think he was at least as comfortable as I was, maybe even more."

Feed community helpers (3+, 7+, 13+)

If you don't want to host a big event, consider bringing food to people who serve the community. You can show your appreciation to them by dropping off a casserole at the firehouse or a tray of baked goods at the police station. It's a nice little thank you for those working long hours on the weekend and holidays to keep us safe. Don't forget to add a pitcher of lemonade in the summer or a thermos of hot chocolate in the winter!

Sheltering the Homeless

On a single night in January 2017, almost 17,000 people in families were living on the street, in a car, or in another place not meant for human habitation, according to statistics from the National Alliance to End Homelessness. Another seven million were living doubled up with family or friends because they didn't have a home of their own, a situation that often leads to outright homelessness. (See the National Alliance to End Homelessness report, The State of Homelessness in America 2016, available at endhomelessness. org, for more information.) These numbers do not include children in foster care who, by definition, are living temporarily in resource homes or facilities.

Raw numbers such as these can be disheartening. But remember, the Christian response to homelessness—and all large-scale social problems—is first and foremost a personal one. Here are some ways your family can help.

Serve with Family Promise (7+, 13+)

Family Promise is a national organization that provides housing, meals, and other services for families with children under the age of 18. Overnight housing sites rotate among different local places of worship throughout the year. Volunteers are needed for driving, at evening meals, and during overnight hosting (at the place of worship, not your home). For more information and to see if this ministry is available in your community, see familypromise. org.

Saint Spotlight: St. Frances Xavier Cabrini (1850–1917)

Feast day November 13

St. Frances Cabrini was born weak and deemed too frail to join a convent. So she and six friends started their own, the Missionary Sisters of the Sacred Heart of Jesus.

Dreaming of going to China as a missionary, she appealed to Pope Leo XIII for permission, but he sent her west, not east. She and her small congregation ended up ministering to poor Italian immigrants in New York City. She founded 67 schools, hospitals, orphanages, and other institutions across the U.S. and throughout the world.

"I will go anywhere and do anything," she said, "in order to communicate the love of Jesus to those who do not know him or have forgotten him."

Pack a bag for a child in foster care (7+, 13+)

Children in the foster care system are often shifted from resource home to resource home with their belongings lagging behind, lost in the mix or shoved in a trash bag. Your family can work with organizations such as Together We Rise and pack fresh, reusable duffel bags, build a birthday box to help the child celebrate his or her birthday, or help build a bike for a child in the foster care system. Do it as a family, or work with your parish youth group or as part of a parish family ministry group. Learn more at togetherwerise.org.

Visit or help a homeless shelter (7+, 13+)

A good way to help the homeless is to volunteer with your local homeless shelter or agency. To locate the nearest one, visit homelessshelterdirectory.org.

Do your homework: Before visiting in person, check out the organization's website or call and talk to a volunteer. Visit on your own before bringing your whole family. Talk to staff about volunteer opportunities, and whether their facility is appropriate for young volunteers. Homeless shelters and transitional housing centers vary greatly. Some are large and institutional; others, such as many Catholic Worker houses, are smaller and informal. (You can find a list of Catholic Worker houses at catholicworker.org. Note that these homeless shelters are run independently by individuals and are not formally affiliated with the Catholic Church.)

"I remember being required to volunteer at the Catholic Worker house in college. That was an experience. It wasn't the work so much as being exposed to a variety of people that my small town just didn't have. You knew they were homeless, and some had mental issues. I was definitely out of my comfort zone on that one, but I still learned a lot."

When you serve in a homeless shelter, keep in mind that often the most important service you can provide is to simply connect with the people staying there—listening to their stories, playing cards, or just sharing a meal with them.

You don't necessarily need to have direct contact with the people staying at the shelter in order to help. Your local organization might also need volunteers to make hygiene kits, do skilled maintenance and repair work, serving in the kitchen, and more. Many shelters post their volunteer and donation needs on their website; your older kids might like to be responsible for checking that list and suggesting ways for the family to help.

Sleep out for the homeless (13+)

For older children and adults looking for more understanding of homelessness, sleep-out events in some communities raise funds and awareness of the challenges of being homeless without even indoor shelter. In selecting a sleep-out activity for your child, as always use discretion regarding supervision. Better yet, volunteer to participate with your child to better continue the conversation at home when the event is over. Discuss how their greater understanding and compassion for the homeless can lead to action in some way, either in serving or advocating for adequate housing. If your community does not have a sleep-out event, consider organizing one. If one family organizes an event for twenty families, maybe half of those families will take what they learn and follow through with some act of service for the homeless.

Saint Spotlight: Satoko Kitahara (1929–1958)

Feast day: January 23

A descendant of Samurai warriors and born into Japanese aristocracy, Satoko Kitahara devoted her short adult life to serving poor slum-dwellers.

After Tokyo was leveled by firebombing and her country defeated in World War II, she converted to Catholicism at age 20 and began serving the garbage-pickers of a slum called Ants Town. She eventually gave up her material comforts and lived with the people she served.

Known as "Mary of Ants Town," Kitahara said, "I experienced a desire to serve ... which seemed a natural accompaniment to being a follower of Christ."

She died from tuberculosis at age 29. Upon recognizing her heroic virtues, the first step to sainthood, Pope Francis declared her venerable in 2015.

Help a ReStore (7+, 3+)

Volunteering at Habit for Humanity building sites is an activity usually limited to teens and adults. Many communities, however, host a Habitat for Humanity ReStore, where you can donate and purchase household building materials, with the proceeds going toward Habitat's building projects. Next time you do a home improvement project, consider donating your old gently-used materials or your half-open box of unused tile to a Habitat ReStore. For more information, see habitat.org/restores. (Expert home improvement hint: Visit the ReStore before you start your project because you might find a really fun mirror or neat light fixture that you wouldn't usually splurge on, for a great price!)

Disaster-related assistance (13+)

When the news tells us of terrible natural disasters around the world, we wish we could do something to help. But often families in our own communities need help in their own disasters. Fires and floods, tornadoes and hurricanes can mean that families face sudden homelessness, lack access to basic resources, and more. Businesses, particularly small local businesses, can be hit hard. Even for those with insurance, the benefits only go so far, and the recovery usually lasts much longer than the outside help. Certainly you can give to fund-raisers for those affected, or even organize one. But personal warmth and help—making a meal, offering to have someone stay at your home while they are seeking permanent housing, helping with cleanup and repair of damages on their property—can also be critical. It will be a lesson not lost on your kids.

"Adopt" a college student (3+, 7+, 13+)

Graduating from high school doesn't mean that a student no longer needs support. Many college students travel far from home to continue their education. If you live in a college town, look for an opportunity to take a college student under your wing. An occasional home-cooked meal and care package during finals week might be the thing that keeps them going. International students who can't go home over breaks especially appreciate this. If you are of the same faith, you can help the student keep in touch with their faith community during this time in their lives.

> "The closest relationships I formed during college were with church families who took me home for lunch on Sundays, had me join their family for an occasional sleepover, and took me grocery shopping before I had a car. They were truly my second families."

Sponsor a refugee or immigrant family with your parish (3+, 7+, 13+)

Catholic Charities USA, through its member agencies in many dioceses, offers a variety of support services to refugees attempting to resettle in the U.S. after facing war, persecution, or threats to their lives in their home countries. Consider working with your parish to sponsor a refugee family through your local Catholic Charities, offering the practical help, friendship, and connections that will enable them to adjust to their life in what is to them a strange new land. Some dioceses coordinate volunteers to help staff set up apartments for refugee families by moving supplies and furniture. Older children and teens can help. These programs also need ESL (English as a Second Language) teacher volunteers and after-school tutoring for children. Your younger children can create "welcome cards" for children of refugee families to get the entire family involved.

Visit the Sick

For much of its history, good Christians have cared for the sick when no one else would. While much of that work has been professionalized by modern healthcare institutions, there are still plenty of ways your family can offer care and comfort for the sick and the vulnerable. Here are a few ideas.

Take care of kids in need (3+, 7+, 13+)

Kids have some unique needs. They have very little control over the challenging situations they face. They are less able than adults to understand why they may be without things and experiences that other children have. By connecting with known groups, such as the following, you assure that many children get help, rather than just a few. New families to the community, including immigrant populations, also are often directed to these organizations.

Ronald McDonald House

Located near most major hospitals that serve children, these houses provide temporary homes away from home for children and families facing long-term hospitalization or requiring daily medical treatment. Ronald McDonald Houses rely on volunteers to host meals, provide special activities, and more. They also accept donations of pop tabs, blankets for children living in the home, and care packages for families, as well as simple snacks to help families get through long days at the hospital. For more information and to find a local house, visit rmhc.org.

Crisis pregnancy centers

Organizations such as Birthright International (birthright.org), active in hundreds of centers in the U.S. and Canada, support low-income individuals and families in bringing their children into this world. Many collect layettes to distribute to those who may not have enough money for blankets and clothing. They offer financial help to women and families facing hardship during pregnancy. Many food shelves do not have diapers or baby food, but these much-needed items can add up quickly for families, and may be offered by a crisis pregnancy center. If your community does not have such a center, contact your closest hospital with maternity services and ask if they have a donation program to help low-income babies that are delivered at their location. The hospital may be able to put you in touch with a local group that is organizing donations or give you information on what is most needed and how to donate it.

Toys for Tots

Hosted by the Marine Toys for Tots Foundation, every December this organization provides new books and toys for children in low-income families. During the season of Advent, take your children Christmas shopping for a child in need. You don't have to give them a large budget, even $5–10 can buy a new book, puzzle, or toy if you shop wisely. You may also host a donation site or volunteer to process donations at a local warehouse. Find more information and a local donation site at toysfortots.org.

Back-to-school drives

Many communities host drives to collect backpacks, lunch boxes, and school supplies for children from low-income families. In addition, schools often have a system for distributing extra supplies to teachers to supplement what students are unable to provide for themselves. Due to limited budgets, teachers frequently end up providing supplies purchased with their own personal finances to support students who need materials. When you are back-to-school shopping with your family, pick up a few extra packages of pencils, crayons, and glue sticks to share with a local drive or your child's teacher. Or ask teachers at your child's school what they need most for students.

Saint Spotlight: St. Marianne Cope (1838–1918)

Feast day: January 23

German-born St. Marianne Cope immigrated to the United States as a little girl and later became a member of the Sisters of St. Francis in Syracuse, New York. She was sent to live and work with people with Hansen's disease (commonly known as leprosy) in Hawaii at an intake hospital. She advocated for the rights of people with Hansen's disease, and addressed governmental abuse head on. She also set up resources and infrastructure to support those suffering from the illness, including a shelter for children of parents with Hansen's disease.

"We will cheerfully accept the work," she said in response to an assignment that she knew would keep her away from the mainland forever.

Provide respite care and friendship (E, $, 3+, 7+, 13+)

Having a child with special needs (e.g., medical, emotional, behavioral, etc.) is an exhausting journey, both physically and emotionally. It is also a rewarding journey that many parents are humbled and honored to take. Getting to know the specific challenges of a special-needs child in order to offer respite and friendship to parents is a generous, worthwhile use of your time. From lending an extra pair of hands during Mass, to offering a safe place or a person who can watch the child on short notice, to inviting a family with a special-needs child over for dinner, your gift will be appreciated.

Serve the women religious in your community (3+, 7+, 13+)

Women religious take vows of poverty, chastity, and obedience. No, they are not always sick, but they give up so much to be so selflessly vulnerable in total devotion to lives of prayer and service. Send a thank you to a religious order, deliver it in person, or consider donating practical and needed items to a convent or women religious retirement home. The older the population of a community, the more they might also need drivers to take them to and from doctor's appointments. Make yourself available for a few appointments with a simple call and scheduling.

Advocate for the unborn (E, $, 3+, 7+, 13+)

Human life is sacred because from its beginning it involves the creative action of God and it remains forever in a special relationship with the Creator, who is its sole end. God alone is the Lord of life from its beginning until its end: no one can under any circumstance claim for himself the right directly to destroy an innocent human being. (*Catechism of the Catholic Church,* #2258)

As Catholic Christians, we respect the dignity of every human person from conception to natural death. You can read more on the Church's full teaching on abortion in the *Catechism,* #2270–75.

We also know that the unborn are vulnerable in our society and need love, care, and advocacy. Here are some ways to serve the unborn, and your local pro-life groups probably organize events of their own of which you can be a part.

Marches and walks for life

Held annually in Washington, D.C., the March for Life gives individuals and families the opportunity to gather with others to advocate for unborn children and for vulnerable women who believe the lie that abortion does not kill a baby. The Walk for Life is also held on the West Coast annually. Consider a family trip to the March for Life or volunteer to organize a trip for your community!

40 Days for Life

Held twice per year (during Lent and in the fall) at abortion facilities around the world, 40 Days for Life is a peaceful prayer vigil. As new members of a parish, I volunteered to take a shift with my four children (ages 1–7 at the time). We had a small campaign site, and we were the only volunteers for our hour. I planned ahead with books, audio rosary, and activities. But I have to admit that it's tough with the youngest kids. One week at the vigil, on the feast of Our Lady of the Rosary, we strung candy rosaries and then stopped at our parish to deliver them to the Dominican priests and brothers. For more information, and to see if there is a campaign in your community, visit 40daysforlife.com.

Volunteer and donate to a local crisis pregnancy center

Most communities have crisis pregnancy centers that provide support for vulnerable mothers. Some centers accept donations of gently-worn business attire, toys, packages and diapers, and formula. The centers on occasion also will host seasonal celebrations for the women they support; call to see how you can help bring a little festivity and levity to mothers facing difficult decisions and challenges ahead.

Work with a nursing home or senior facility (E, $, 3+, 7+, 13+)

Visit family or friends

Perhaps you have a family member or friend in a nearby nursing home. You may already have a regular schedule or routine for stopping to visit. Creating that kind of schedule of visits is an easy way to serve with a broad mix of children's ages. If your own family members are too far away to visit, you can stay involved in their care by sending a care package now and then. Come with your children throughout the year to trick-or-treat, with Valentines cards, an Advent wreath, Christmas cards, you get the idea. A small handmade token of love or gesture of thoughtfulness will make a great impact.

"When our friend had a new baby, my mommy made them supper and my brother made lemon bars and juice. I made a big, big card for them with my little sister."

Adopt an individual, a floor, or a unit

If you don't have family or friends in a nursing home, you may visit someone who does not receive many visitors (all too often, the majority of the residents). Call the nurse manager or volunteer coordinator before visiting so they can suggest someone who needs visitors, and you can learn about any special rules.

Consider adopting a floor or unit and getting to know the residents there. Then you can care for them as you would your own family through visits, letters, and even small gifts.

Perform music or do an activity

When visiting a nursing home, particularly to visit a non-relative, it's good to have a plan for your visit. You could arrange a musical performance to give your children a chance to practice and build their performance skills in front of an appreciative audience. You can also plan an activity, such as Play-Doh, craft projects, card games, board games, or reading aloud.

Even if the residents you visit don't do the craft or play with the Play-Doh, younger children will usually open up and be more conversational with an activity in front of them. Seeing the young people engaging in activities in their common space is beneficial for older populations even if they don't participate. Some places use the more active technologies of Wii for bowling and other sports that residents previously enjoyed. Your older children may enjoy doing that with them.

Help with technology

Older people increasingly turn to technology such as Skype and e-mail to keep in touch with distant family members. However, learning to use a computer or tablet can be tricky, especially when the keys are small and the type on the screen is difficult to read. Providing technical support is a great project for teens who want to help out. Offer to help in a nursing home. Or find a community bulletin board in a senior apartment complex or an assisted living facility and post a time when you will be available to help.

Make a blanket for someone undergoing chemotherapy treatments (3+, 7+, 13+)

Cold sensitivity can be one of the side effects of undergoing chemotherapy. Making a tie blanket out of two pieces of rectangular pieces of fleece is easy to do, practical for people needing the extra warmth, and a good way to say "I care." Contact your local hospital or cancer treatment center to see how and where to donate the blankets. They might set you up with an already organized group that exists to make sure blankets stay germ-free for recipients. WikiHow has easy-to-follow directions and video to help you and your child make the blankets: wikihow.com/Make-a-Fleece-Tie-Blanket.

Be a reading or study buddy ($, 13+)

It would be wonderful if all children grew up in a home where they had help with their homework and were read to each night before bed, but unfortunately, many children do not. Due to many obstacles such as illiteracy, language barriers, work schedules, and health issues, to name a few, some parents (even those who want to) can't help their children with schoolwork. Check with your local library or school district to find a program that works with children who are struggling academically. You and some of your older kids could read or study with such children. If you can't find a local program, you could start one!

Visit the Imprisoned

As I mentioned in part I, visiting prisons with your young children is nearly impossible. However, it IS possible to visit people who are imprisoned by their personal financial circumstances, health, mobility issues, or life situation. They are homebound or otherwise confined without freedom to play and live safely.

Be a mother's helper (E, $, 13+)

You and your children could well become a real hero to the mother or father of small children who need a break.

- Offer to visit and keep small children entertained while mom or dad get work done (or takes a nap!).

- Or offer to babysit so that parents can attend appointments and run errands unencumbered by little ones.

- Accompany parents to Mass, adoration, or appointments to help with little ones.

Spring and fall yard cleanup (E, $,7+, 13+)

When I was on extended bed rest during one of my pregnancies, it was beautiful to see how many people from our parish and community showed up to help us with yard work. One of the fall work camp groups from our parish came and spent an afternoon helping my husband. The young members of our community not only helped with physical labor but also took time to play basketball with my kids. Sometimes I think that was the greatest service they provided—spending some one-on-one time with my kids.

Find a neighbor or elderly member of your parish who might have a hard time finishing these spring and fall jobs, and volunteer to come over with your children for an afternoon

"Our Lord does not look so much at the greatness of our actions, or even their difficulty, as much as the love with which we do them."

—St. Thérèse of Lisieux

to help out with whatever cleanup they need done. This is a great activity to do if you decide to start a service club (p. 90).

Visit and bring a homemade gesture in collaboration with Eucharistic ministry (E, $, 3+, 7+, 13+)

Usually organized through your parish or a hospital chaplain, Eucharistic ministers bring Our Lord in Communion to those who are confined to home, the hospital, or a nursing home. Only trained Eucharistic ministers may offer the host, but younger children can make cards and draw pictures for those you will be visiting. Older children may be able to accompany you on the visit, too, depending on the circumstances. Similarly, if you are not a Eucharistic minister, offer to make homemade tokens of thoughtfulness for Eucharistic ministers to gift while they are visiting homebound people.

Give kids a safe place to play (7+, 13+)

Some children do not have the opportunity to play freely in a safe environment. Many cities have programs such as the Fresh Air Fund which will connect families who reside in safe communities to host children who need the space to safely and simply be children. Learn more at freshair.org. Other cities have programs that offer at-risk children safe and free after-school, before-school and summer camp opportunities such as the Boys and Girls Clubs of America. Contact your local affiliate to fill direct needs, which may include sponsoring with your service group a holiday party, learning activity, or a special "Day for Kids."

Drive someone to church (E, $, 3+, 7+, 13+)

Do you have extra room in your car? Many people feel imprisoned by their inability to drive due to their age, illness, or disability. Drive someone to church who cannot drive themselves independently. Some parishes coordinate driving people with severe disabilities who live in residential facilities or nursing homes to weekly Mass. Added bonus: you and your family can sit with that person at Mass and eventually include them in your weekly Mass routines. Maybe you go out for a special treat after Mass? Maybe, over time, you can include your new friend, too.

Work with your diocese to help a family who has an incarcerated parent ($, 13+)

Many dioceses have active prison ministries and are seeking volunteers. Many of these positions are best suited for adults. However, reach out to your diocese's prison ministry and see if you can connect with a family who has a parent in prison. Those families need extra support during a stressful time. It might be something simple like they need a few home-cooked meals or help with childcare so that the family member at home can visit the family member in prison.

Take on human trafficking and child labor (E, 7+, 13+)

Do you know who made those shoes on your feet? Who picked the fruits and veggies that grace your dinner table? It might not seem like there is not much we can do about forced and child labor in places far away. We can, however, educate ourselves and advocate for ethical options. Check out your family's slavery footprint at slaveryfootprint.org. Commit to making informed choices when possible, and praying for the victims when you can't. For example, shoes are expensive and in a large Catholic family they can certainly add up quick! Finding an ethical option can be a financial impossibility. Instead, commit to pray for the person who made your shoes every time that you put them

Saint Spotlight: Blessed Stanley Rother (1935–81)

Feast day: July 28

Father Rother grew up on a family farm and liked getting his hands dirty. Not the best student, he almost didn't become a priest because of his challenges with learning Latin. But he had a great way with making friends, and he used his farming skills to help the poor farming communities of Guatemala. Despite his troubles with Latin, he learned two languages to become part of the community there. He tended to the sick, taught the community about Jesus, and helped them build an irrigation system to support better crop production.

He knew if he stayed in Guatemala that he was risking his life, but he refused to abandon his community. The first martyr born in the United States, he was murdered in 1981 after being falsely accused of getting involved in the dangerous and violent political conflict there.

on and teach your children to do the same.

For more ideas on fighting human trafficking, check out the list compiled by the U.S. State Department: state.gov/j/tip/id/help.

Sex trafficking is a form of human trafficking that particularly affects young people, and sex trafficking is fueled in part by pornography. You can team up with an organization called Fight the New Drug to fight the prevalence of pornography by joining their "Fighter's Club" or getting involved in one of their campaigns. See their website for more details: fightthenewdrug. org.

Finally, consider teaming up with WE.org to learn about and fight child labor. The organization was founded by Craig Kielburger who, as a twelve-year-old boy, formed a student-led movement to end child labor. You can learn about his story and get your kids involved at the organization's website.

Carol at a prison or court-ordered rehabilitation facility ($, 7+, 13+)

Some court-ordered drug rehabilitation facilities will welcome singing groups. Contact a local facility, particularly those that house mothers and their children in drug rehabilitation programs, to see if your family can sing Christmas carols or do arts and crafts with the residents there.

Visit a homebound person (E, $, 3+, 7+, 13+)

Poor health, age, disability, or lack of transportation are just a few factors that may prevent people from regularly getting out of their homes. Homebound people may not be imprisoned, exactly, but reaching out to them surely counts as a work of mercy—namely, visiting Christ in prison. Here are some ways to reach out.

Meals on Wheels

Meals on Wheels delivers lunchtime meals to homebound residents during the week. Volunteers drive a route, usually with five to ten stops, to deliver meals that are prepackaged and labeled. Younger children can make cards or place mats to deliver with the meal at each stop. Older children and teens can bring the meals to the door. Mom or dad can drive! For more information on Meals on Wheels programs in your neighborhood, visit mealsonwheelsamerica.org.

Improve access to healthy food, clean water, and opportunity (3+, 7+, 13+)

Some communities are imprisoned by the systemic obstacles that keep them from flourishing and receiving the many things others take for granted. Here are ideas of how your family can reach families from other parts of the world and provide them opportunities to thrive.

Give hope through gift catalogs to those around the world

Every year at Christmas my parents "gift" my children a dollar amount to spend on farm animals, training, and implements for families in developing nations. From an organization's catalog, they can each choose an animal that helps support a family for the dollar amount they are given, or they combine their gifts to purchase a more expensive animal. Choosing life-changing gifts for others teaches children not only generosity but also about the lives and challenges of people around the world. An organization with an excellent track record in this is Heifer International at heifer.org. Beatrice's Goat, a book recommended in the resources for talking about hunger and thirst, is based on the work of Heifer International.

"My mother-in-law works with a mission in Sudan. She's been able to share her experiences visiting Sudan and bring to life the situation of real people there. My kids have seen pictures of the people she met, and my oldest sometimes reads the monthly newsletter we receive. This helps them understand how valuable a school, a well, or a bicycle is—and how we take them for granted."

Catholic Relief Services

In addition, Catholic Relief Services, at crs.org, the official humanitarian aid organization for the U.S. Catholic Church, has a gift catalog with opportunities to "buy" health services, access to clean water, education, job training, farm animals, gardening supplies, and so on.

Catholic Relief Services has outstanding programs of aid, development, and service worldwide. Many parishes participate in their annual Rice Bowl program during Lent. This campaign provides ways to learn about other countries' needs, to try meatless recipes from other cultures, to practice Lenten sacrifice and almsgiving by donating to CRS' programs, and to have conversations around your table based on daily reflections. For more information, visit crsricebowl.org.

Host a garage sale for people around the world

Rather than having mom or dad simply write a check for a donation, have children do chores or host a garage sale and donate the proceeds to Catholic Relief Services or any other organization that works to enhance the well-being of people around the world.

Host a fair trade sale at your parish or community gathering

Catholic Relief Services partners with an organization, Servv, to bring fair trade crafts, coffee, and chocolate to people who want to buy from artisans and farmers around the world, while giving them a fair price for their goods. Your family can order these useful, beautiful, delicious, and reasonably priced items through a catalog, or online at crsfairtrade.org/crafts. If you like what you see online, you might organize a consignment sale at your parish, or get friends and family together to place a community order. Information on hosting a consignment sale or a community order is on the above web page.

Bury the Dead

Funerals are as much a learning opportunity as a service project. While your family is helping prepare or serve the funeral meal, your children will be learning about the Catholic understanding of death and dying. Even if they have little or no interaction with the grieving family, they will understand the process better when they eventually face the death of one of their own loved ones.

I think of serving at a funeral as one of the best multi-age activities, not because the entire family can serve together doing the same job, but specifically because they probably can't. Younger kids have a chance to see much of the planning and work that go into funerals and to participate in new and interesting ways as they grow. Being able to "graduate" to a new level of service within the same project helps children and parents appreciate how they're growing through service.

Serve a funeral meal (E, $, 3+, 7+, 13+)

When our daughter died, a friend called and told me that her girls had volunteered to help with the food service during the funeral. It was lovely to see such familiar young people in the kitchen helping out and taking care of the job. Another child from the same family helped serve Mass with our son. We were happy to donate the leftover cookies and bars back to the parish to be enjoyed by the confirmation students!

Make place mats or table decorations

Even before children are able to assist in the kitchen or with serving the funeral meal, they can make place mats or decorations for it. They may simply decorate blank place mats (be sure to talk about appropriate decorations), or older ones can do something more crafty. Simple centerpieces featuring a photo of the deceased, if you have access, can provide conversation starters for the grieving and a tangible memorial gift they can take home with them.

Food preparation

Even though many funerals take place during the school day when children can't be there, elementary-age{hyphenated like school-age} kids are often capable of preparing a simple dish or assisting with a more complicated one. Some parishes use a phone chain or email blast to notify people when food is needed. Be on their list!

Kitchen work

Volunteers set tables, organize food, cut desserts into individual servings, etc. When the meal is finished, someone has to box up the leftovers, wipe down the tables, and take out the trash. Parishes may have a committee that rotates this responsibility, so check with the office to find out how to get your family in the rotation.

Honor a baby who has died (E, $, 7+, 13+)

When our oldest daughter died in 2007, we wanted to do something special to honor her memory. So we asked friends and family to donate their favorite grief and loss books. On what would have been her first birthday, we delivered a new lending library of books for children and adults to the bereavement program at our local hospital.

Such a memorial drive is a great activity, but you can also honor a baby who has died in other simple ways. If your family has lost a child to miscarriage, stillbirth, or infant death, consider having the baby's name added to one of the registries for the unborn. (See below). Both registries are free—although donations are welcome and appreciated—and open to people of all faiths. If you have a friend or family member facing this hardship, share with them the registry websites. Or offer to submit their child's information on their behalf, then send them a card letting them know that you followed through, with information on the registry you chose.

- Shrine of Our Lady of Guadalupe, guadalupeshrine.org/pray/naming-the-unborn-memorial

- Church of the Holy Innocents, Shrine of the Unborn, https://shrineofholyinnocents.org/shrine-of-the-unborn

Care for Our Common Home

Pope Francis has called on Catholics to care for the environment in our daily lives to ensure that it is protected not only for future generations, but also for those affected most by climate change and environmental destruction: the poor (p. 19). Thankfully, this unofficial work of mercy gives us many opportunities to serve as a family, integrate caring for the environment into daily life, and to get outdoors!

Reduce, reuse, recycle (E, $, 3+, 7+, 13+)

Within your family, teach the practices of "reduce, reuse, recycle." At home, recycle, conserve water, turn off the lights, and use the air conditioner less (or not at all). Make it fun to see all the ways you can cut down on waste in your family's life.

If you have a math-minded middle-school-aged child or teen, show them the electric or water meter in your house, have them track your family usage for a few months, and see what it takes to reduce your family's consumption. Some libraries and community organizations offer devices, which can be checked out just like a book, to plug into wall outlets to measure usage. Also consider your family's vehicle usage. Are there places you usually drive that you could walk or bike to instead? Can you use public transportation? You may not think of these practices as service, but they are in fact serving the earth that sustains us.

"Glance at the sun. See the moon and the stars. Gaze at the beauty of earth's greenings. Now, think. What delight God gives to humankind with all these things…! All nature is at the disposal of humankind. We are to work with it. For without we cannot survive."
—St. Hildegard of Bingen

Small gestures to take care of the environment go a long way. Consider using beeswax wraps instead of plastic wraps and reusable bags and containers for storage and shopping. These items can be purchased online or homemade from recycled fabric. Decorate parties and events with reusable or biodegradable paper decorations. Ditch the balloons and use paper lanterns instead. Do not offer your guests plastic water bottles, use paper cups. These small changes will make a huge impact on our landfills, waterways, and environment.

Dispose of electronics properly

When electronics no longer work, the best place for them is not the trash. Certain kinds of batteries and light bulbs should not be trashed either, but recycled. Teach your kids that landfills can be dangerous places because chemicals and other toxins can leach from the circuitry into the ground. If your city or county has a system for recycling electronics, make a flyer that you and your children can post around town to help educate others. Consider a letter to the editor explaining the importance of proper electronics disposal. If your community does not have a specific program, do some research and find the closest drop site. See if there is a way that you can create a drop site that is more easily accessible to people.

"My parents owned a custom lawn mowing business. Every week, we donated our time to mow our church's lawn. Before we were old enough to operate equipment, we helped pick up trash that had blown in, swept clippings off the parking lot, and pulled weeds around flowerbeds."

Use smart guidelines for fostering plant and animal life

When you learn to identify an invasive plant, pull it up from the roots and dispose of it by guidelines provided by regional agencies. If you like to hunt and fish, know and follow all state regulations in order to properly maintain animal populations. Each state's department of natural resources usually has websites with excellent resources.

Beautify your community (E, $, 3+, 7+, 13+)

Have you ever considered that making a place beautiful is a type of service? Think of it as environmental hospitality!

Take care of parish or religious community grounds

Who takes care of the grounds at your parish? Is the job paid or is it handled by volunteers (more likely)? Who cleans out the landscaping each spring to keep things beautiful? Volunteer with your family to help if it's needed. Or help with seasonal cleanup and/or building maintenance for a religious community.

Main Street

Many small businesses, nursing homes, and other community locations have landscaping that needs refreshing each spring. Often those flower boxes you see outside the dentist's office are a pet project of one of the employees or one of the patients. Without that person volunteering, those small touches might never happen. If you live in a town with a defined main street, consider building a collection of small flower boxes that businesses can place outside their main entrance. Beautify Main Street and build a relationship with your local businesses at the same time!

The cemetery

Take the time to deliver flowers from a wedding or a funeral to your cemetery, focusing on the graves that may not get much attention. You can call a local florist and request that unwanted flowers be saved for this purpose (or to deliver to a hospital or nursing home). The reverse of decorating the cemetery is assisting with fall cleanup, removing decorations before the snow falls. You might want to place flags at graves on Memorial Day. In addition to beautifying your community, you are also honoring the deceased with your prayers and presence.

"The last two years we did spring cleanup at the shrine. We have a group of middle-school students, and they basically clean for the day. Two years ago we even had two groups. One group went up and cleaned the church, and the other group cleaned the basement and meeting room. Last year we did the entire church (pews, brass, etc.) and outdoor yard cleanup. It was easy to get them to do the work without complaint, and they could see how, with the effort of the larger group, we accomplished a lot. They are mostly excited to go each year. Being away from school, doing something different, they see results or feel like they are making a difference."

Take care of a road, beach, public playground

As a family, take responsibility for a section of road that you can easily reach, a playground where you frequent, or a beach you visit. During an evening walk with kids, take a few moments to clear the drains and bring a bag for any trash you find. Maybe when your neighbors see you working they will be inspired to do the same. Plan ahead and bring bags and a wagon to haul trash (you might be surprised at how much you find). If you're not close to a water source to wash hands immediately, bring along some plastic gloves, wet wipes, and hand sanitizer.

Care for animals in need

Animal shelters are often looking for volunteers to feed and walk animals, and to spend time giving love and attention to them. The more socialized the animals in the shelter are, and the more accustomed they are to being around a variety of new people, the more likely it is that they will eventually be adopted.

Plant a tree

Celebrate Arbor Day by planting a tree (or two or three) each year. Find out when Arbor Day is celebrated in your state; it varies according to the states' planting seasons. Trees provide food, shade, and shelter for people and animals. As plants, they are involved in photosynthesis, making our air healthier. Trees prevent wind and water erosion. At certain times of the year, some organizations provide free or reduced-cost trees for those who are willing and able to plant them.

Create a creation care team in your family and/or with your parish ($, 7+, 13+)

Ask older children to make a poster to sketch ways that your household can reduce waste. Discuss electricity and utility usage with your children. Walk, ride bikes and scooters, use public transportation, and carpool more frequently if possible to reduce your family's carbon footprint.

Catholic Climate Covenant

This organization gives parishes ways to make a direct impact on their environment through their parish-wide Creation Care Teams. Work with other families in your parish to create a team that:

- sponsors parish-wide events to celebrate and learn about caring for the environment, such as on the feast of St. Francis,
- reduces parish plastic water bottle usage,
- reduces parish electricity waste,
- encourages bike riding and walking through the community rather than buses if possible,
- releases paper lanterns instead of Mylar balloons for memorials, and
- decorates at parish events with biodegradable and reusable materials.

The website provides a wealth of resources and can be accessed at catholicclimatecovenant.org.

Visit a farmers' market (E, 3+, 7+, 13+)

The local farmers that you meet at area farmers' markets are typically excellent examples of land stewardship and environmental health. Support their efforts by purchasing food for your family directly from these farmers. If you visit the market regularly, you may get to know some of the vendors better and have the opportunity to visit their farm and learn more about sustainable farming practices.

Collect scrap metal to collect money for charity (E, $, 13+)

Here's a way to care for our common home and donate to your favorite charity: Collect scrap metal, sell it to a scrap metal yard, and save that money for charity. It can be a messy (and potentially dangerous job), so make sure your older kids are ready with gloves and elbow grease. Earth 911 has the basics to get you started, including a list of scrap yards near you: earth911.com/eco-tech/basics-recycling-scrap-metal-money.

Adding to Our Gifts with Prayer

Sometimes we aren't able to serve another person directly (although I hope this text has challenged that idea), but we can always serve another person with our prayers. For more information on praying with your children, see the Peanut Butter & Grace guide, 77 Ways to Pray with Your Kids. This list can help get you started with service-oriented prayer in the meantime.

Holy hour for religious liberty (E, $, 3+, 7+, 13+)

Does your family attend adoration on a regular basis? Can you commit to spending one hour per month praying for those who face religious persecution in our country and around the globe? Many parishes are now setting aside a specific time for this purpose, but even if yours is not, you can still use any adoration time for this. Maybe there are others in your parish who would join you in dedicating a special hour for praying for religious liberty.

Pray for priests (E, $, 3+, 7+, 13+)

Priests do a lot of hard work for all of us, and it is often somewhat thankless. Commit to praying for your parish priest or another priest you know for a period of time, and then be sure to let them know by sending a quick thank-you note.

Pray for foreign missionaries (E, $, 3+, 7+, 13+)

The Catholic Church has missionaries, both lay and religious, around the world doing incredible works of service as a part of their daily life and calling. Pray for those who have made serving others their life's work. Ask around your church and community for the name of a specific individual or family you could pray for by name. Consider corresponding with that person to ask for specific prayer requests and needs.

Spiritual bouquets

Commit to praying for priests, missionaries, or those who serve others daily during a particular liturgical season. At the end of the season, bless them with a basket of goodies and a note with all of your prayer intentions. Make a simple spiritual bouquet using construction paper and simple shape cutouts to create a bunch of flowers. You might do this project as a part of a service club, and have each person bring a predetermined number of items for individuals you have been praying for. On the day of your group's gathering, fill the baskets and make cards for each of the people you have been praying for.

Serve your parish ($, 7+, 13+)

Most parishes rely extensively on volunteers to help the staff in ministry roles, not to mention more mundane tasks. Many parishes send annual "Time and Talent" surveys to ask families in which ways they could serve. If you receive such a survey, fill it out with your kids. Here are some of the activities you might consider:

- being an extraordinary minister of the Eucharistic or a lector
- counting money after Mass
- being an altar server
- ushering or being a minister of hospitality
- hosting the coffee hour after Mass
- preparing the altar for Mass
- presenting the gifts at the altar during Mass
- helping with seasonal liturgical decorations
- doing janitorial work
- helping with mailings
- teaching or assisting with religious education classes
- helping with youth ministry events
- participating in music ministry
- participating in funeral ministry

Most of these jobs are limited to older children and teens (some require reception of the sacrament of Confirmation); others, though, can be done by whole families together.

Serve without Leaving Home

Sometimes it's not practical to do the works of mercy outside the home: illness, lack of transportation, the temperament of our little ones, or our own energy level create impediments. Fortunately, there are many ways your family can serve others from the comfort of home.

Teach a new skill (E, $, 7+, 13+)

Help your kids learn, refine, and then teach others skills that they can use to serve others. Begin by thinking of a skill you have used to serve others in a regular way. Are you the go-to person in the office when there is a computer problem? Do you regularly give away zucchini every summer? Teach your child whatever useful things you know. Some examples might include cooking, cleaning, gardening, handcrafting (sewing, knitting, etc.), woodworking, carpentry, automobile maintenance, computer operation, and home repair.

Host a party for a charity (E, $, 3+, 7+, 13+)

In lieu of gifts for a birthday, holiday, or anniversary party, consider asking attendees to donate to a charity. Collect canned goods, baby diapers, or cash. Instead of party favors, donate to a charity on behalf of your guests. With planning you might be able to arrange a field trip to give your donations to the charity together.

Write a letter (E, $, 3+, 7+, 13+)

When we can't reach out to someone personally, writing letters enables us to reach out in another way. About half of the New Testament consists of letters, mostly from St. Paul to the early Church communities. These letters offered instruction, insight, and encouragement. If Paul thought letter writing was important, the rest of us should probably pay attention!

Thank-you notes

Letter writing can be as simple as coloring a picture or sending an extra holiday greeting, un-birthday card, or surprise note to a friend or family member. Thank-you notes help others feel appreciated for their hard work or thoughtful gift. Sending thank-you notes can turn an attitude of gratitude into an activity of service.

Beyond friends and family, consider those who work in community service fields—such as police officers, firefighters, and EMTs—as possible letter recipients. With young children, use a form letter so they can dictate their favorite part of a certain gift, or have them color a picture inside a preprinted note. Slightly older children can fill in the blanks on a form letter and sign their names. By the end of second grade, most children can write short thank-you notes independently. But it's never a bad idea to have a family habit of thank-you note writing together, so it doesn't become a chore.

Opinion letters

Older family members can write a letter to the editor or a letter to a politician to speak out about Catholic social justice issues or specific local needs. Older children and teens can participate actively in the political system by corresponding with their legislators even before they have the right to vote. In addition to sending notes about local issues or pending legislation, perhaps your teen could draft a thank-you note to a local politician for a position they have taken, particularly when the decision to do so involved one of those tough Catholic social teaching issues. Challenge yourselves to reach out at least once a month through the art of letter writing.

Sponsor a child (E, 3+, 7+, 13+)

Through child-sponsorship programs, families sponsor a child by providing monetary support for that child and his or her family. The child usually writes to the sponsoring family several times a year, and the sponsoring family is invited to write letters as well. Unbound, Caritas for Children, and the Christian Foundation for Children and Aging are all Catholic organizations that run child-sponsorship programs.

One way to involve the entire family in such a sponsorship program is to have a list of daily tasks, which, when completed by your child, earns an allowance for the benefit of the sponsored child. Younger children can work together for the same child, while older children might sponsor a child individually with their allowance. An even older child with a job may decide to tithe some of his or her job income in order to sponsor a child.

Sponsorship organizations often randomly match children and sponsors, but many also allow sponsors to select a specific child. Connecting with a child of the same gender and roughly the same age may make the experience more meaningful for the sponsoring child and/or family.

Clean closets and donate (E, $, 7+, 13+)

Make a regular habit for your family of noticing what things around your home are going unused. Do your bookshelves overflow so much you can't even find the books you want to read? Do your closets have more clothing that you don't wear than clothing you do? Instead of throwing away your unwanted stuff, donate it to a thrift store.

Send a care package (E, 3+, 7+, 13+)

Sending care packages is a way to take letter writing one step further to provide support and encouragement to a person who needs it. When sending care packages of food, necessities, or entertainment items, include handmade cards and/or letters of encouragement.

Here are some ideas for care packages to make.

Door decorations for nursing homes

Making a nursing home feel like home for the residents is a big job, one that often falls to the spare time of staff and the generosity of friends and family. Call a local nursing home and ask how many beds they have. With your kids, create seasonal decorations that are the right size for displaying on the residents' doors. Snowflakes, hearts, shamrocks, flowers, suns, Christmas trees … there are plenty of ideas to last the whole year. Consider laminating the door decorations and including a dry-erase marker for writing residents' names. This way, the decorations can be used for several years before being replaced.

"Our church's first through fourth graders wrote letters of encouragement and thanks to a missionary family working in Nepal. Though we couldn't send a care package—infrastructure after the earthquake didn't support this—it was a good opportunity to talk with the kids about what missionaries do and how a written note can lift spirits."

Depending on the facility, nonreligious decorations may be preferred out of respect for the diversity of the residents. Mail the blank decorations (include tape or poster tack) to the nurse manager or volunteer coordinator, who can have someone hang the decorations on each door. Better yet, bring your care packages to your local nursing home yourself.

This is also a great way to stay involved with family members who live in a nursing home that is too distant to visit regularly.

Military care packages

Active-duty military are often separated from family and friends for extended periods of time. Care packages have long been a way that people back home can help ease the loneliness and hardships of deployed soldiers.

It's best to work with an established organization to help you meet military and postal delivery requirements, which vary depending on the destination. One such organization is Support Our Troops, which has suggestions for care packages at supportourtroops.org/care-packages.

In addition, many soldiers face extended periods of hospitalization because of combat injuries. Contact your local veterans' hospital for information on corresponding with recovering soldiers.

Presents for hospitalized children

Children's hospitals are often looking for activities to keep their young patients busy. Speak with your local hospital's volunteer coordinator, child life specialist, or nurse manager to find out what they need.

> "The most meaningful parts of sponsoring a child for my children were seeking a child similar in age, from a high-risk country, and then sending and receiving real letters from the child. Knowing that a child from the other side of the world shares similar interests has a great impact on intercultural awareness."

If your local hospital is open to your ideas, you might suggest sending coloring books and crayons or other art supplies, simple craft kits with easy-to-follow directions, bubbles, book bags (full of books, of course!), travel-size puzzles or puzzle books, and gift cards to nearby shops and restaurants.

Stuff a stocking (3+, 7+, 13+)

At the beginning of December we celebrate the real-life St. Nicholas, Bishop of Myra, with his generous heart toward those in need and his love for children. Introduce your family to the real St. Nick and then bless an organization with gifts for their clients during the Advent season. Use small stockings and fill them with goodies for those in need. I've included a few suggestions to get you started, but be creative and solicit more ideas from your kids. Stocking stuffing is another fun activity you might do with a service club (p. 90).

For animal shelters

Show respect for God's creation by surprising the four-legged critters living at the local humane society with dog treats, collars, small cat toys, tennis balls, small blankets, and more.

For hospital patients

Being stuck in the hospital is never fun, but it is especially difficult during the holiday season. Consider stuffing your stockings with lip balms, lotions, crossword puzzles or simple activity books, small project kits, simple holiday decorations, and more.

For wounded veterans and soldiers

Many of the ideas for hospital patients are also applicable for veterans. In the care package activity (p. 74) is a website address that gives information about sending packages to those serving in the military overseas.

For homeless shelters

Stuffed stockings can be a fun way to package hygiene kits around the Christmas season. Toothbrushes, travel toothpastes and other toiletries, a new washcloth, and more are appreciated.

Random acts of electronic kindness (E, $, 13+)

Online reviews

These can literally make or break a business, especially in competitive industries such as hospitality services. If you have a positive experience at a hotel, restaurant, or a favorite local store, take the time to leave a review. You'll make someone's day. Don't forget to review your favorite authors, either—it may be the biggest "payment" they get, and reviews on book selling websites such as Amazon and Goodreads make a big difference. Even young children can be involved in leaving short reviews for their favorite titles. Feedback also helps smaller publishers (like Peanut Butter & Grace!) have better ratings and circulation, boosting exposure online.

Contribute to a positive social media environment

If you and/or your teen are using social media, work to create a positive environment by sharing uplifting memes, blocking negative people and groups, and liking pages that support your family goals and values. As a Catholic person, consider using social media to get to know a religious order. Teach your teens how to keep their social-media house as "clean" as their actual house. This might not seem like an act of kindness, but with all of the online interactions that happen in a day, contributing to a positive climate can literally bless thousands of people in one day.

Just a reminder, each family should carefully discern the appropriate timing and use of social media sites by teens. There are real risks to online interactions for our children, including early unintended exposure to pornography. For more information and ideas, check out the Peanut Butter & Grace article, "5 Steps to Help Protect Your Teens Online."

Organize a new project on DoSomething.org (13+)

Do Something is a social justice site for young people by young people. It is basically a social media community to organize campaigns in areas of need identified by the participants. Recycling clothing, creating birthday cards for homeless kids, and even providing tech support for seniors are among the wide variety of opportunities for young people to make connections through service. Some of the campaigns are location specific, but most encourage action in the person's own community. Parent caution: dosomething.org/us is an open social media site, and as such, children and teens should approach with caution and a parent close by. Not all of the projects will be appropriate and some may be outright contrary to Catholic teaching. For older teens this is a great way to infuse some quality Catholic social justice into a mainstream environment. For younger kids, it might be better to pass on the website itself until they are a little older!

"Jesus taught his disciples to pray by asking the heavenly Father not for 'my' but for 'our' daily bread. Thus, he desired every person to feel co-responsible for his brothers so that no one would want for what he needs in order to live. The earth's produce forms a gift which God has destined 'for the entire human family.'"

—POPE BENEDICT XVI, ANGELUS, 12 NOVEMBER 2006

PART III: REFLECTING

While it is possible to stop after learning more about the works of mercy and doing a few simple activities, that is only part of the process if you want to fully teach your children the importance of service. The final section of this book on reflecting is meant to help you integrate the activities and their meaning more fully into your family life. Sometimes reflecting may be as simple as a family discussion over dinner or sharing the experience with a friend and inviting them to join you next time. The more intentional your family is about reflecting, the more you will be building family culture and attitudes that will endure long beyond each individual activity.

It may surprise you to find a section on Catholic Social Teaching at the end of the book rather than the beginning. Remember that this book is about the Cycle of Service. What was necessary to prepare for your early service activities has changed, and in reflecting on this experience you will be preparing for your next.

Your child most likely learned about the number three by first seeing, touching, and tasting it ("three cookies, please!"), but imagine the holes in their education if no one ever came back to teach them what a *three* looks like! Don't be tempted to skip this section as optional. In many ways it is the most important for your family in the long run and forms the foundation for everything that happens in the heart of your children moving forward.

Immediate Intentional Reflection

The first reflection that needs to happen is the immediate processing of your experience as a family. This can happen in the car on the way home or at the dinner table the next day, but it must happen, ideally in the next 24 hours. Ask each family member to share their highs and lows from the service activity.

- What went well and what was hard for them?

- What did they see, experience and learn?

- What questions do they have after the experience?

- What feelings do they feel after the experience?

- Is there anything that you need to consider if you are going to repeat this activity in the future?

- How did they see Jesus in the people that they served?

Consider sending a thank you note to the organization or group that you worked with to show your appreciation for the opportunity to serve.

Make a note of any adaptations your family would like to make to the activity, further areas of study, and follow up action and activities that you would like to complete. The next section on Catholic Social Teaching will help you with any specific study you would like to complete. In this way, your reflections from one activity will naturally lead into your preparation for future activities.

Revisit the related questions and information from "Talking about the Tough Stuff" in part I.

This doesn't need to be formal and scripted but it does need to be intentional, in that it needs to ensure that the experience is thoroughly addressed through both positive and negative aspects, and that every person in the family has a chance to have their voice heard and questions answered.

Reflect Throughout the Liturgical Year

B elow are examples of how your family can integrate reflecting on service in your daily lives with concrete affirmation of your children's works of mercy. May they be small daily tasks or mighty service projects, it is good to see through visual aids that they make a difference.

Celebrate a liturgical season (E, $, 3+, 7+)

The liturgical seasons of Advent and Lent offer many opportunities for service within the home. Here are a few ideas.

Advent: A bed for Baby Jesus

During the season of Advent, help your child prepare a soft bed for the Baby Jesus. Place an empty box or manger in a special place in your home. Each time your child does an act of service for another person (big or small), add a small piece of yellow yarn ("straw") in the manger. (If space is an issue, post a drawing or collage of a manger on the wall, drawing in the yarn or gluing it onto the picture.)

Then, after your child goes to bed on Christmas Eve (or while they are in the car waiting to go to the vigil Mass), place Baby Jesus in the soft bed prepared by your child's actions.

As kids get older, be sure to point out that while the manger scene is symbolic, their actions really and truly welcome Jesus into their hearts.

Lent: Bean jar

Everyone loves jellybeans for Easter! Dried beans ... not so tasty. Throughout Lent, add a dried bean to a large glass jar each time you observe your child doing an act of service. Point out that these acts of service are one of the ways kids can participate in the Lenten practice of almsgiving.

On Easter morning, replace the dried beans with jellybeans to enjoy for an Easter treat.

Lent: Crown of thorns

Make a clay or dough ring and stick toothpicks in the clay; Crayola air clay works well, as does oven bake or polymer clay. When your children are "caught" in an act of service, have them remove a toothpick (if you bake the clay you will need to break them off). On Easter morning, decorate the crown of thorns—which, if things go well, is now without a thorn—with flowers. Use it as a centerpiece for your Easter table to show the beauty of the Resurrection that always follows the sacrifice of the cross.

For any time: Good Deed Beads and Heartprints

Good Deed Beads, also known as Sacrifice Beads, are basically nine or eleven beads threaded on a length of cord or string in such a way that the beads stay in place when a child moves them from one end of the cord to another. The idea is that the child keeps track of his good deeds and/or sacrifices for Jesus by moving the beads from one end to the other throughout the day. If you make an eleven-bead string, it can double as a one-decade rosary. A nine-bead string doubles as a way to pray a novena. You can find links to examples on the Peanut Butter & Grace Pinterest page.

Heartprints is a children's book by P. K. Hallinan (Ideals Children's Books, 1998) that describes how our acts of kindness can leave an impression—a "heartprint"—on others. After reading the book with your kids, write each child's name on a large piece of poster board. Cut out some hearts from colored paper; whenever a child is "caught" leaving a heartprint, he or she gets to paste it on the board using a glue stick. Get a more detailed description of this activity at pbgrace.com.

Praying it Forward

The more time your family spends in active service, the more aware of community and individual needs you will become. Remember the noticing game from part I (p. 41)? If you have been practicing, your kids are probably getting pretty good at it by now, and they are going to want to do something about everything they see. It may be tempting to tell them that you can't, but the truth is that God gives us an extra special way to work on those situations we can't personally affect … and that's prayer!

Find a spot in your house to keep a centralized prayer list for your family. It could be a special bulletin board or chalkboard set aside for requests, or it could be a notebook that is kept in a common location. At our house, we use our prayer board to put birth announcements, funeral cards, and have post it notes available to write individual requests. I also keep a separate notebook with a master list with more room to share updates as we have them. Whenever possible include photographs or other images that can help younger family members "read" the list themselves. This could even be a picture of the building or homeless shelter where your act of service took place in order to remind your child of the person or activity involved. Even the youngest kids can be the greatest prayer warriors with the right tools!

Catholic Social Teaching

The deeper that your family digs into service, the more appealing and meaningful it will become for your children to grasp the Catholic teachings on various social issues.

When teenagers begin learning how to drive, they start with the basic rules and then practice driving with an experienced adult. They receive learners' permits while they practice the laws and rules of the road. We know that the day they finally receive their coveted licenses, the learning is not over. They still have etiquette to learn, and in many states, their licenses come with restrictions for a period of time. There is a balance between learning the rules they need to drive and getting them behind the wheel to experience it for themselves and then fully mastering their skills. For the purpose of this book then, there are some basics of Christian Service, which were covered in part I of the text, that are necessary to get behind the wheel in part II. Knowledge of Catholic social teaching is not "extra" or "optional," but it does make more sense and is easier to learn after having had some experience behind the wheel.

For Catholics, acts of service are informed not only by the Gospel, but by the Church's teaching on social issues. The Church has always offered direction about how to apply the principles of Jesus' teaching to social issues, but the modern Catholic social teaching tradition really started with Pope Leo XIII's 1891 encyclical *Rerum Novarum* (on capital and labor). (An encyclical is a letter to the whole Church.) In it, he addressed the pressing social problems of the day, especially the conditions of the working poor, and proposed how the Church, following the teaching of the Gospel, might respond.

> **Saint Spotlight: Blessed Irma Dulce Pontes (1914–92)**
>
> *Feast day: August 15*
>
> Born into an upper-middle class family, young Irma couldn't ignore the poverty she saw. At the age of thirteen, she began caring for the poor in her own neighborhood, giving haircuts and treating wounds. At eighteen, she joined a Franciscan order; a few years later, she began housing the sick and homeless in the convent's chicken coop. Today, it is a 1,000-bed free hospital, and the charitable organization she began is the largest in Brazil.

Subsequent popes and conferences of bishops have continued to connect the dots between the demands of the Gospel and the social conditions of modern life, addressing topics as varied as economics, international relations, family life, human dignity, poverty, civic life, the arms race, and the environment. Together, these social teaching documents provide a plan or road map for achieving the common good—that is, the state in which all people can fully realize their God-given potential.

A basic knowledge of Catholic social teaching can enrich your family's experience of service in several ways, by directing you to pressing areas of need you would not have otherwise considered, guiding the way you serve, providing insights into the larger social context of your service experience, and helping you to make connections between your family's experience and the faith it professes. More importantly, knowledge of the Church's social teaching might someday help your family move from acts of direct service to action promoting justice on a larger scale.

There are many excellent resources available for learning about Catholic social teaching; you may find some of them in your parish library, but if not, an Internet search for the term "Catholic social teaching" will yield many possibilities. Two resources are worth highlighting.

First, the United States Conference of Catholic Bishops maintains an excellent collection of articles, activities, and introductory videos on the Catholic social teaching page on its website, usccb.org. Additional books, pamphlets, and videos are available for purchase from USCCB Publishing. The website also provides extensive background on particular issues under its "Issues and Action" tab.

Second, the Vatican's 2004 documents, the Compendium of the Social Doctrine of the Church, systematically summarizes Catholic social teaching through 2003. It's available both as a printed book and online at the Vatican website. While it is pretty dry reading and beyond all but the most precocious kids, you might find it a helpful starting point for learning about Church teaching on particular issues.

A consistent theme of Catholic social teaching is the option or love of preference for the poor. Today, this preference has to be expressed in worldwide dimensions, embracing the immense numbers of the hungry, the needy, the homeless, those without medical care, and those without hope. (St. John Paul II, **Solicitudo Rei Socialis** [1987], #42)

Building Community through Service

Once upon a time, belonging to a community was essential: Neighbors relied on one another for mutual aid, assistance, and protection because the institutions that provide those things today didn't exist. Now, many people are isolated from even their closest neighbors, not only by the institutionalization of service, but by the proliferation of modern conveniences: air conditioning, automobiles, conversation-squashing lawn mowers, in-home entertainment, the Internet, and cell phones. Sometimes, it takes a real crisis for people to rediscover the joys of community.

Connecting with your local community has several benefits:

- Communities in which people have strong connections with one another tend to be safer, healthier, and happier than those in which people are isolated and disconnected.

- Connecting with others in your community may reveal hidden opportunities for doing works of mercy that you might not otherwise notice. Once you are on a first-name basis with the elderly couple down the street, for example, it becomes much easier to check in and help if you see an ambulance visit their house. And once your kids get to know the kids down the street, it's more likely you'll know to help out when that family comes down with the flu, has a baby, or experiences a layoff.

- Connecting with others in your community can provide your family with allies and collaborators for doing the works of mercy. If a neighbor breaks her ankle and needs help for a couple months, for example, you can organize a meal train with other neighbors. Or you might find yourselves collaborating on issues that affect the whole community, such as the need for safety improvements along your street.

- Once others in your local community are connected with you and your kids, your kids will be safer out and about in the neighborhood because other adults will be more likely to watch out for them or to help if they get into trouble.

- As you get to know and help others in your neighborhood, it is more likely that they will reach out to help your family, too.

As you reflect on your service experiences, use this opportunity to promote a spirit of community. Here are some bonus family activities for intentionally building or forming communities, especially in your neighborhood.

Make a neighborhood map and directory (E, $, 3+, 7+, 13+)

Take your older kids (ages 5+) on walks around your neighborhood, and help them map all of the residences, drawing a box for each one. Try to fill in all the boxes with the names of the people (and pets!) who live there, and if possible, contact information. If you don't know many of your neighbors, this may be a long-term project. Take your map along with you, using the project as a pretext for introducing yourself and your children to the neighbors you meet outside. You can then enlist your neighbors' help completing it.

Alternatively, you might enlist your neighbors' assistance in creating a neighborhood directory that can be distributed to everyone who participates.

Organize a neighborhood party (3+, 7+, 13+)

A neighborhood or block party isn't as much work as you might think it would be, and it's a fun way to get to know new neighbors and reconnect with neighbors you haven't seen in a long time. If you like, recruit a couple neighbors to help you. Here are some tips:

- The first time you plan your party, plan ahead by three months or so to allow enough time to get things organized and to get the word out. If you make it an annual tradition, it will be easier in subsequent years.

- Choose a date that typically has good weather and fewer insect issues (e.g., wasps) in your area. Sunday evenings might be an optimal time because families that have been away over the weekend are more likely to be home. You may want to coordinate your event with the National Night Out, the first Tuesday in August each year, a project of the National Association of Town Watch.

"The neighborhood party I organized with a couple other parents has become an annual tradition. Ten years out, everyone knows just what to do and what to bring, so it's hardly any work at all. Plus it's a great way to meet the new families who move into the neighborhood!"

- Have a backup plan in case of inclement weather—either an indoor location, or a cancellation plan.

- Call the city to apply for a permit to close the street. Check to see whether the city has a program supporting neighborhood events; some municipalities will send first responders or park and recreation staff to set up games.
- Make "save the date" flyers to distribute to neighbors a month before the event.
- Put up a few yard signs to remind people of the date and time. Your local print shop can help with these.
- Consider hiring a musician or just providing music from a portable stereo.
- Make it pot luck! Everyone can bring their own dish to pass, as well as utensils and place settings and seating. It's a neighborhood party, so people can always run home if they forget utensils.
- Provide an icebreaker activity, or some pretext for people to mix and meet new people. Google "Human Bingo" for a really easy icebreaker activity.
- Consider inviting local politicians, too.

See "Plan a Neighborhood Block Party" at pbgrace.com for more ideas.

Form a babysitting co-op (E, $, 13+)

If you have younger children, form an informal neighborhood babysitting cooperative so that you and other parents can easily swap kids on short notice. Check in with older residents who may be willing to watch kids, too.

Welcome the stranger (E, $, 3+, 7+, 13+)

Make a special effort to welcome new arrivals in your neighborhood with a welcome basket or a sweet treat. Also make a point of introducing yourselves to new members of your church community. Set a family goal to greet one new person every Sunday!

Go trick-or-treating in your neighborhood (E, $, 3+, 7+, 13+)

Halloween offers a built-in opportunity to meet the neighbors. Although curated events at schools and churches have become popular in recent years, make a point of at least visiting your immediate neighbors—especially older residents who may especially enjoy seeing your kids in costume. Nursing homes and hospitals also frequently offer trick-or-treating opportunities.

Christmas caroling (E, $, 3+, 7+, 13+)

Christmas caroling in your neighborhood is another fun way to meet your neighbors and build community. This is an activity you can do as a family, but it will be more fun if you gather a few other families to go with you. Contact friends, neighbors, or place an announcement in your parish bulletin.

Caroling can also be a work of mercy, especially if you plan to visit an institution for those in need, such as a soup kitchen, homeless shelter, hospital, nursing home, or county jail. Alternatively, contact your parish for the names of homebound individuals, and go caroling at their homes. You'll need to contact the volunteer coordinator for these institutions a few weeks in advance.

Community service days (3+, 7+, 13+)

Community service or volunteer days are organized for one day each year by a specific group to encourage volunteering throughout the year. Colleges often organize days for faculty, alumni, and staff. Volunteers select an activity for that day from a list of projects. Cities, schools, and banks are also known to organize days for entire communities. Watch for local events and make a family commitment to participate in the next one you see.

Volunteer while building skills

Youth organizations such as 4-H develop children and young people through mentoring and the acquisition of considerable practical skills. Along the way, they also give youth and their families opportunities to participate in community-based volunteer projects. See 4-h.org.

Walk or run for charity

If you have an active family, or even if you don't, you might enjoy participating in a walk or run event to raise money for a specific cause. Such run or walk events generally donate a portion of entry fees to a specific cause. Some encourage additional donations through the creation of teams, which raise money for their own particular causes.

If you complete a run or walk as a family, enjoy the process of preparing together. Maybe even take time to decorate hats or shirts that you will all wear. Take pictures and keep them around to remember what fun it is to serve together!

Neighborhood watch (E, $, 13+)

Work with your local police department to set up a neighborhood watch. Besides improving neighborhood safety, it's another way to connect with your neighbors. Older kids and teens can participate in the watch meetings. The National Crime Prevention Council has tips at its website; search for "neighborhood watch" to find it.

Start a Service Club

Family is only one group of people that can serve together. Do you have a group of families from your parish, or friends or neighbors, who may be interested in serving together? Once you have experienced the cycle of service for yourself, go deeper by organizing a service project for the group of your choosing. Fundraisers or collection drives are particularly well suited for larger groups, but all of the activities in this book could be done with friends. Doing projects with friends can help spread out the cost and time commitment of some activities to make them easier and help them reach more people. Your family may only be able to make holiday cards for a small unit in the local nursing home, but with the help of other families you can set a goal to bless all of the residents in that home!

We have a small group of local Catholic families we get together with for fellowship and learning from time to time. We've done several service learning projects as a group, but my favorite was our Lenten Spiritual Adoption Campaign. Throughout Lent each family offered prayers for our local priests and made flowers or other notes of their prayers. The week before Holy Week we got together and made cards and packed gift baskets. The kids brainstormed to create the list of priests that would receive the baskets and made the cards in groups. Each family brought ten of some item they thought a priest would enjoy. We had homemade jellies, candy, trail mix, and a variety of other small treats. We distributed our spiritual bouquet flowers between all the baskets and each family delivered one or two baskets during Holy Week.

Here are steps to starting a service club:

1. Choose a project.

2. Make a lists of what you will need and who you will invite.

3. Set a date.

4. Send invitations, including what each family needs to bring and any transportation needs.

5. Host your project.

6. Do any follow-up activities, such as delivering items if needed (include the group whenever possible).

7. Send thank you notes to everyone who participated and any organizations that hosted your group.

8. Start planning the next event.

Final Thoughts

Your biggest question at this point might be, what can I do today? The most important part of this book is not which projects you decide to complete. Some activities simply may not be available in your area or are not a good match for your family for a variety of reasons. There are also seasons in life when serving others might take a back seat to addressing family situations or concerns. I encourage you to cultivate an attitude of service during those times by serving each other, serving others with your prayers, and continuing to grow in knowledge and understanding. The time will come for your family to step out in service again.

In his historic address to a joint session of the United States Congress, Pope Francis said of the refugee crisis, "We must not be taken aback by their numbers, but rather view them as persons, seeing their faces and listening to their stories, trying to respond as best we can to their situation."

I truly believe this is true not only of the refugee crisis but also of situations right in front of us. There will always be more that we can do. There will also be more people in need of our generous care and human compassion—in need of a helping hand. As Christian families, it is our duty and our responsibility to reach out our hands to hold up the dignity of the families and individuals right in our midst in our local communities.

My great hope is that you will take the ideas in this book and make them your own. Find what projects spark joy in your family, make memories, and encourage further action. Then find opportunities to build on that to develop your own family culture of service. By including a diverse sample of activities, I have aimed to help your family find the activities that are the best fit for you. In writing this book, I often found myself challenged by knowing that there is so much more I could be doing. Could I ever do enough? The answer is probably not, but that doesn't mean I shouldn't try.

That being said, the more projects you try, the more likely you are to find the issue or type of service that sparks your family's passion. Even if you find right away that your family members really are drawn to working with the homeless, for example, make an effort to try other types of service as well. Use the index as a checklist of activities for motivation if you find yourself in a rut with ideas. In trying more, your entire family will benefit from a greater understanding not only of our diverse society, but also of the diverse needs of its people.

APPENDIX: RESOURCES

Books

Arganbright, Becky. *The Little Flower: A Parable of St. Thérèse of Lisieux* (picture book). Peanut Butter & Grace, 2015.

Ajmera, Maya. *What We Wear: Dressing Up Around the World*. Charlesbridge, 2012.

Brother Lawrence of the Resurrection. *The Practice of the Presence of God*. Image Books, 1977.

Buckley, Colleen. *Grandma Kathy Has Cancer*. Dog Ear Publishing, 2007.

Burr, Wesley R. et al. *Sacred Matters: Religion and Spirituality in Families*. Routledge, 2011.

Carlson, Natalie Savage. *The Family Under the Bridge*. Harper Collins, 1989.

Curley, Terence P. *Six Steps for Managing Loss: A Catholic Guide Through Grief*. Alba House, 1997.

Daughters of St. Paul. *Spiritual & Corporal Works of Mercy* (coloring and activity book). Pauline Books and Media, 2003.

Davison, Kenneth. *Corporal and Spiritual Works of Mercy: How God's Love Transforms Your Heart* (children's book). Holy Heroes, 2018.

DePaola, Tomie. *Nana Upstairs and Nana Downstairs*. Puffin Books, 2000.

Disalvo-Ryan, Dyanne. *Uncle Willie and the Soup Kitchen*. Morrow Junior Books, 1991.

Ernst, Kathleen. *Caroline's Secret Message*. American Girl Publishing, 2012.

Judge, Lita. *One Thousand Tracings*. Disney-Hyperion, 2007.

Kerley, Barbara. *A Cool Drink of Water*. National Geographic Children's Books, 2002.

Libreria Editrice Vaticana. *Catechism of the Catholic Church*. USCCB, 1997. Second Edition.

Lovasik, Lawrence G. *The Works of Mercy* (picture book). Catholic Book Publishing, 1983.

Nelson, John. *The Little Way of Saint Thérèse of Lisieux*. Liguori Publications, 1998.

Martin, Chia. Rosie: *The Shopping Cart Lady*. Hohm Press, 1996.

McBrier, Page. *Beatrice's Goat*. Atheneum Books for Young Readers, 2001.

McGovern, Ann. *The Lady in the Box*. Turtle Books, 1999.

Milway, Katie Smith. *The Good Garden: How One Family Went from Hunger to Having Enough*. Kids Can Press, 2010.

Peterkin, Allan. *What About Me?* Magination Press, 1992.

Pontifical Council for Justice and Peace. *Compendium of the Social Doctrine of the Church*. USCCB, 2005.

Pope Francis. *Laudato Si: On Care for Our Common Home*. USCCB, 2015.

Prenatal Partners for Life. *Our Baby Died and Went to Heaven*. 2009.

Schnurbush, Barbara. *Striped Shirts and Flowered Pants: A Story about Alzheimer's Disease for Young Children*. Magination Press, 2007.

Shriver, Maria. *What's Wrong with Timmy? Little Brown Books for Young Readers*, 2001.

Stickney, Doris. *Water Bugs and Dragonflies: Explaining Death to Young Children*. Pilgrim Press, 1997.

Taback, Timms. *Joseph Had a Little Overcoat*. Viking Books for Young Readers, 1999.

Trottier, Maxine. *A Safe Place*. Albert Whitman & Co., 1997.

Weber, Kerry. *Mercy in the City*. Loyola Press, 2014.

Wellborn, Amy. *Loyola Kids Book of Saints*. Loyola Press, 2001.

Williams, Karen Lynn, and Khadra Mohammed. *Four Feet, Two Sandals*. Eerdmans, 2016.

Windley-Daoust, Jerry. *77 Ways to Pray with Your Kids*. Peanut Butter & Grace, 2015.

Websites

Birthright International: birthright.org/en

Boys and Girls Club of America: bgca.org

Catholic Charities USA: catholiccharitiesusa.org

Catholic Climate Covenant: catholicclimatecovenant.org

Catholic Relief Services: crs.org

Catholic Volunteer Network: catholicvolunteernetwork.org

Catholic Worker: catholicworker.org

Church of the Holy Innocents, Shrine of the Unborn: shrineofholyinnocents.org/shrine-of-the-unborn

Do Something: dosomething.org/us

Earth 911: earth911.com/eco-tech/basics-recycling-scrap-metal-money

Family Promise: familypromise.org

4-H: 4-h.org

40 Days for Life: 40daysforlife.com

The Fresh Air Fund: freshair.org

Habitat for Humanity Restore: habitat.org/restores

Heifer International: heifer.org

Meals on Wheels: mealsonwheelsamerica.org

National Alliance to End Homelessness: endhomelessness.org

National Study of Youth & Religion: youthandreligion.nd.edu

Peanut Butter & Grace: pbgrace.com

Ronald McDonald House: rmhc.org/ronald-mcdonald-house

Shrine of Our Lady of Guadalupe, Naming the Unborn Memorial: guadalupeshrine.org/pray/naming-the-unborn-memorial

Slavery Footprint: slaveryfootprint.org/

State Department: state.gov/j/tip/id/help

Support Our Troops: supportourtroops.org/care-packages

Together We Rise: togetherwerise.org

Toys for Tots: toysfortots.org

WE Families: we.org/we-families

WikiHow: wikihow.com/Make-a-Fleece-Tie-Blanket

Work and Play, Day by Day: workandplaydaybyday.com

Online Articles

Pope St. John Paul II. "Homily in Perth, Australia," 1986. Retrieved at w2. vatican.va/content/john-paul-ii/en/homilies/1986/documents/hf_jp-ii_ hom_19861130_perth-australia.html

Roberto, John. "Best Practices in Family Faith Formation," Lifelong Faith, Fall/Winter 2007, pp. 21-38. Retrieved at lifelongfaith.com/up-loads/5/1/6/4/5164069/lifelong_faith_journal_1.3.pdf

ACKNOWLEDGMENTS

As in all projects, this has been a labor of love. It is not a labor that was undertaken alone, however. Most importantly, I must thank my family for letting me hide in my office for long periods of time and for putting up with my constant stream of, "You know, we should really do this …" While I would love to tell you they are all as enthusiastic about service as I am, I have to admit they (and I) sometimes wonder if I might have gone too far with this, that, or the other suggestion. They also picked up more than their share of work around the house when I started getting sucked into the project.

Secondly, I'm grateful to all the friends and family who helped make this project a reality. In particular, I kept calling and texting Leigh and Lisa when I needed "just one more idea" for a particular section … which almost always turned into a series of "just one mores." Thanks also to all the blog readers and friends who submitted recipes and ideas and offered their service stories so generously.

Finally, thank you Jerry for saying "yes" on the back of a chance meeting and to Barbara & Regina for all of your hard work getting this project to the finish line. You were all unendingly patient with my inexperience and have influenced my writing for the better.